HAVANA AND OTHER MISSING FATHERS

CAMINO DEL SOL

A Latina and Latino Literary Series

HAVANA AND OTHER MISSING FATHERS

Mia Leonin

THE UNIVERSITY OF ARIZONA PRESS
Tucson

The University of Arizona Press
© 2009 Mia Leonin
All rights reserved

www.uapress.arizona.edu

Library of Congress Cataloging-in-Publication Data

Leonin, Mia.
Havana and other missing fathers / Mia Angela Leonin.
    p. cm. — (Camino del sol)
ISBN 978-0-8165-2815-8 (pbk. : alk. paper)
1. Havana (Cuba)—Description and travel. 2. Cuba—
Description and travel. 3. Leonin, Mia—Travel—Cuba.
4. Leonin, Mia—Family. 5. Fathers and daughters.
6. Women poets, American—Biography. 7. Cuba—
Biography.
I. Title.
F1799.H34L46   2009
917.291'230464—dc22
                2009007536

Publication of this book is made possible in part by the
proceeds of a permanent endowment created with the
assistance of a Challenge Grant from the National Endowment for the Humanities, a federal agency.

♻

Manufactured in the United States of America on acid-free,
archival-quality paper containing a minimum of 30% post-
consumer waste and processed chlorine free.

14 13 12 11 10 09   6 5 4 3 2 1

Epigraph credit: Excerpt from "For My Father," which appeared
in The Triumph of Achilles; reprinted in The First Four Books of
Poems, by Louise Glück. Copyright 1968 to 1995 by Louise Glück.
Reprinted by permission of HarperCollins Publishers.

Book composition: David Alcorn, Alcorn Publication Design

This book is dedicated to my mother, Norma Jewel Leonin,
To the memory of my father, José Ignacio Alsina,
And to my daughter, Rafaela Emanuelle Ochoa

FOR MY FATHER

I'm going to live without you
as I learned once
to live without my mother.
You think I don't remember that?
I've spent my whole life trying to remember.
—LOUISE GLÜCK, FROM *THE TRIUMPH OF ACHILLES*

Por fin sola, armoniosamente sola.
—FROM *LA VIDA ES SILBAR*

Contents

Acknowledgments

First, thanks go to Celeste Fraser Delgado, whose invitation to Bogotá, Colombia, set me on this very important journey. And to Elizabeth Cerejido, *hermana de alma*.

I am indebted to the following people who read the manuscript at critical junctures and provided invaluable feedback: Celeste Fraser Delgado, Shara McCallum, Martha Otis, and Maxine Weaver. Silvia Wilhelm made a meaningful journey possible. Thanks to the following friends for their feedback, encouragement, and guidance: Catherine Bowman, Ever Chávez, Juan David Ferrer, Mark Koven, Anne Tschida, and Thomas Williford. A special thanks to the Ragdale Foundation, whose fellowship and residency allowed me the time and space to complete this project. Many thanks to Patti Hartmann, Kristen Buckles, and Nancy Arora for their support.

I am deeply indebted to my mother, Norma Jewel Leonin, for her courage and love. Finally and most importantly, I thank Carlos Ochoa, *compañero constante, infatigable apoyo—te amo*.

Except for those of my parents and my friend, Liz, the names in this book have been changed.

HAVANA AND OTHER MISSING FATHERS

Norma

(Prologue, 1967)

She slips from her room on Denmark Street, past her mother twitching in her dreams, her father feigning sleep. She releases the emergency brake, and her '65 Ford convertible groans beneath the weight of her possessions: two satin-covered overnight cases and three dark green garbage bags, dumped into the trunk like mounds of soil. She lets the car roll halfway down the block in neutral before turning the ignition. It's seven and a half blocks to Churchill Downs, outside Louisville, then over the Ohio River, into Indiana, and through a quick stretch of Illinois. By noon, she'll have crossed the Missouri line. She'll stand in front of the nursing director with little makeup on, fingernails scrubbed and bleached, her calves and thighs shrouded in thick, white support hose. She'll stand up tall, bracing herself against the child in her belly, an invisible weight curled around its thumb.

It's February 1967. She's thirty-five years old. The sky hangs low over the quiet interstate and buildings locked up for the night. As the car rumbles past downtown Louisville, she catches a glimpse of the vanilla-colored brick of Kentucky Baptist Hospital where she took her nursing training. The chill of the metal steering wheel pierces through her maroon leather driving gloves. As she crosses the Ohio River into Kentuckiana, the bridge and downtown skyline recede in her rearview mirror like a barge disappearing on the horizon.

Her landscape has always been the cloud-colored, rain-soaked eaves of her neighbors' houses on Denmark Street, the sturdy grid of front porches perched three steps from the sidewalk, and the backyard chicken coops, churning out their combustion of feathers and grime. Now, she's crossed the river, passed the last exit. The possibility of Ohio is behind her. She checks her face in the mirror. Is this really the woman who's going to Missouri? Is this the one who *must* go to Missouri? After a few hours, Indiana deflates into a nondescript stretch of Illinois, and finally, the St. Louis Arch, the clogged arteries of traffic, and on to farmland—endless fields of soy, corn, and motionless heads of cattle bowing into cement troughs. The expanse of land begins to open up. She's moving west, toward wider, boxier states like Kansas, Iowa, Nebraska, and Missouri.

Every mile that distances her from Denmark Street is a relief, but she determines early on that she will not like country living. The symmetry of land, horizon, and sky strikes her as frigid and confining, and this first impression will never quite thaw. As a teenager, she haunted Louisville's river bottoms where phlegm-throated men hawked fish heads, chipped buttons, and sandwiches of gray cheese. From rickety sale tables and the dented tailgates of pickup trucks, she scavenged for smudged canvas shoes and the bolt of organdy print with the least discernable pick in the weave. Her mother made all her dresses and covered the shoes in the same fabric, so that they'd match. In the city, there was always a way of making something ugly beautiful, but rural Missouri feels pre-set, a hard boot stamped into the frozen earth. Still, she has a job offer. This is her chance for a fresh start.

She accepts the job in the rural town, tacks up curtains made of old skirts. She sleeps on her belly. How alone can one body be when it has another tucked away inside? Spring passes. The child is born. Life resumes. She feeds the child, drops her off at the sitter, and takes herself to work at the state hospital. The woman throws herself into her work. She takes on an extra shift at the hospital, then a weekend job. She tries to keep thoughts of her family at bay: Mother's high-pitched lamentations, Daddy's gentle psalms, their Bible, an inseparable wound and salve.

The child guzzles her milk. She feeds constantly yet is always empty; she eats but is never full. Her unruly hair must be sheared away every couple of months by the coarse hands of the local barber. She eats her beans and scavenges for memory. At first, the woman can satisfy her. She places a stethoscope in her hands, or she slips a record album from its cellophane sleeve, and they form a giggling conga line, the stray dog named Mutt snapping at their heels.

The child watches men carry their daughters from church, the girls sprouting from their fathers' shoulders, as golden and narrow as stalks of wheat. She demands family stories, and the woman obliges by telling anecdotes that barely escape being the truth. In all of them, the woman is dancing. To congas and orchestras, she dances. In some stories, she knows the steps; in others, she must learn them on the spot, but the central image persists: she's swept off to supper clubs—her satin dress cinched at the waist, her cocktail with a paper umbrella twirling inside.

In the woman's version of the past, the girl's deceased father was a doctor—sometimes an internist, other times a psychiatrist or surgeon. The girl pulls his last name behind her like an exotic piece of luggage her schoolteachers can't pronounce. When pressed, the woman calls the girl's father "Jerry" and speaks of him as a good angel, but when the pocket-sized photo occasionally turns up in a drawer or basement box, her voice turns uncharacteristically sharp. She comments that he was selfish, cold, and distant. She names him the source of her daughter's dark moods and fierce stare. This is where the stories always trail off, until one summer just after the girl's sixteenth birthday.

The white Missouri heat looms on the other side of the aluminum screen door. Cockleburs burrow into the scorched yard. The woman slumps over in a powder-blue velvet King Louis chair that juts out from the paper-thin wall, her head hanging heavy in her hands. The news—that she met the girl's father many years after her husband, Jerry, had passed away—lurches from her in deep, retching sobs. The reality that the girl's true father was never dead, just absent, runs down the woman's face in savage streaks of cobalt blue eye shadow and jet black mascara. As her sobs slow, the woman grows quiet. The girl thinks she has dozed off and starts to cover her, but then the retching sounds well up again. The woman shakes slowly, quietly, until her entire body convulses; every inch of her participates in the expulsion of this long-concealed secret.

The smell of dog urine hangs flatly in the air, mixing with the toxic-sweet odor of the cherry-scented candles the woman places in votive cups. The woman has never been able to train the dog or the girl. "Well, at least I'm a good nurse," she always jokes. The girl consoles her; she strokes her hair. She brings tissues and puts cold compresses on the woman's face. She forgives the woman with great decorum—hugs and full-fledged sentences of absolution. She forgives though she's nowhere near forgiveness or even understanding. She can't yet feel her own rage welling up. She wipes the woman's tears, places a final cold washcloth over her eyes, and waits. After a while, the woman jumps up. She pencils on Cleopatra eyes and fresh lipstick. They go to Dairy Queen and say nothing more of the incident. The girl knows better than to ask anything else about her father. He's a Cuban exile, a doctor, who didn't want anything to do with the birth. Anything else she wants to know, she'll have to find out for herself.

At home, they retreat to their respective rooms. The girl sits next to an old wicker basket, her head aching from the ice cream. Although she's always sensed her father wasn't dead, she's not ready for this. The news implodes in her stomach and questions begin to form in waves of nausea. The already tenuous rope connecting the girl to her town and her friends feels frayed to the point of snapping. Being the daughter of a widow is respectable. Although it has felt absurd at times, it is comprehensible, like putting your hand over your heart during the pledge of allegiance. Suddenly, she's the daughter of a foreigner, the daughter of someone who didn't want to be a father.

She rummages around and finds the old stethoscope lying beneath a stack of papers, quizzes, and school photos. As a little girl, she was told the stethoscope had belonged to her father, and she often played hospital with it, imagining her heroic father saving lives. She puts it to her chest. Her heart is deadpan at first, beating steadily over and over, save a trick or two where it seems to skip a beat or wait extra long before fluttering. She moves the stethoscope all over her chest as she's seen doctors do on TV, then on an impulse, she touches the flat metal surface to her stomach. The earpiece explodes and crackles with activity. Waves crash against rocks. Sea salt spews up from the cracks and crevices. The girl spends hours curled up next to a pile of laundry yet to be folded and listens.

Miami International Airport, 1988

I'm twenty. He's seventy-three. I don't have a photo of my father, but I'm certain I'll recognize him. I've spent the bulk of the trip to Miami reveling in my newfound identity of traveler, so when my flight makes a bumpy landing and comes to a screeching halt at the airport in early January 1988, I'm surprised to find myself frozen in my seat, unable to gather my things and disembark. Coat sleeves dangle from the overhead bins and brush my face as sleepy passengers snap to attention and begin filing out around me. I peer into the mirror of my tortoiseshell compact, examining my face in circular fragments—a short, deep scar just outside the corner of my left eye, a tawny-colored mole on my nose. I angle the mirror like a periscope and stare hard into its glassy eye, willing myself leagues beneath this plane's metal gut. I'm not a traveler. I'm a girl from Missouri with a ticket to meet my father for the first time, and I'm terrified.

Only one picture of my father existed. My mother named it "Jerry" and declared him deceased. The black-and-white, wallet-sized photograph inspired wildly divergent eulogies: he was patient and kind; he was cold and self-centered. My father was a psychiatrist, an internist, an ophthalmologist. He was "foreign." He emigrated to Florida, Kentucky, or Baltimore from the Philippines, from Cuba, from some faraway island. The only consistent feature was the dancing. In all the stories, my mother was buoyed from rumba to cha-cha-cha. It swept her from her parents' oppressive house on Denmark Street to clubs with names such as the Iroquois Room or the Louisville Belle.

I start down the wide gangway. For the first time since I began this journey at 6:00 a.m., it occurs to me that I don't know what my father looks like.

My mother and I hefted concrete blocks into the trunk to leverage her Cutlass Sierra against the icy highway and slogged two hours and forty-five minutes to the closest airport, just north of Kansas City. She left, so I waited alone three hours for my flight. I had plenty of time to think of practicalities, but instead submerged myself in the anonymity of the airport. The imagined destinations of the travelers eclipsed any real thoughts of the implications my trip might have. Now, as I watch family members flag each other down or stand in clusters, punctuating their conversations with spontaneous embraces and kisses, I wonder how he will find me. He might have copied one digit in the flight number incorrectly. Perhaps he's standing on the other side of the airport, craning his neck to get a glimpse of any young woman disembarking alone. Before these thoughts can lead to either a practical plan of action or pure panic, I see my father and his wife staring at me. They're several yards away, and I set out in their direction without openly acknowledging them, just in case I'm wrong.

My father stands immobile and silent. His short, stout wife radiates black hair tinted a deep burgundy henna. She talks rapidly, her hands fluttering around him like a pair of nervous birds. She rifles through her purse for something, then turns to brush imaginary lint from my father's gray plaid sports jacket. He's unexpectedly tall. His skin's my color, fair with an olive tone, and his round, watery, hazel eyes stare back at mine, registering the similarity. I hold out my hand. The wife starts snapping photos. She barks out instructions to him in Spanish, and he shuffles closer to me. I still have that picture. There's no other way of saying it: he looks terrified.

Spanish has fourteen verb tenses, English has six. My father and I speak in only one—the present.

"You travel fine?" he inquires, rocking forward just a little on the word "fine."

"Yes, thank you," I smile politely, just as I've been trained to do when an elderly person asks me a question. We wade into the present tense, intoning questions and answers, inflecting simple declarative statements, and preparing to join the chaotic chorus of airport reunions, crashing and careening around us.

Today has been my first time on a plane, my first landing and arrival. I see a family of Hasidic Jews and think they are Amish. I see Cubans for the first time and feel startled and embarrassed to realize there are more of them than just one fair-skinned man buttoned into a wallet-sized photo. Spanish floods the loudspeaker and springs from the mouths of airport workers and travelers. The swallowed *r*'s and dropped *s*'s dip into anonymity then bubble up around me like the family I just watched descend upon a young man sporting a buzz cut and slinging a large canvas duffle bag over his shoulder.

We walk from the gate past a man holding a cardboard sign that reads "Royal Caribbean Here." That's how I've carried my "Cubanness" up until now—like a stark cardboard sign, a piece of information my mother conveyed with little explanation when I was sixteen. But now my father is a few steps ahead of me and his wife farther ahead. I follow him through the Miami International Airport, thinking the MIA tag fluttering on my bag is a good omen. Stepping into a wall of humid night air, hanging on to the broken syllables of my father's English, I feel like I'm on my way. I feel almost close to something.

Papi

By the second day of that first visit in January 1988, I'm calling José "Father," or more precisely, "Papi." Did I step outside, hear some kid yelling after his father, and follow suit, chirping "Papi" like a life-sized parrot? Did I ask my father's wife, Zoraida, the Spanish word and did she reply with the Cuban informal, relegating me to the status of a little girl rather than a young woman visiting her father for the first time? I don't know, but somehow I emerge from that first night of sleep, face scrubbed, stomach rumbling, and a cheerful "Buenos días, Papi" flying from my lips without a trace of irony.

Zoraida and my father stop in mid-conversation. A tall breakfast bar separates the kitchen from the open dining area where an enormous china cabinet sits behind an imposing dining table, plastic azaleas bristling at its center. For the rest of my visit, my father and I will eat all our meals at the breakfast bar while Zoraida cooks, cleans, serves, and pops morsels of food into her mouth from the other side.

My father asks me how I slept, and I reply politely that I slept just fine. He pauses to formulate a question.

"You want cornflake?"

"Yes, thank you," I reply, my words setting Zoraida into action. Her movements burst with energy. She vigorously shakes the cornflakes from their box, briskly slices a huge ripe banana, and pours whole milk into the bowl with the limber wrist of a bartender. In Miami, even a bowl of cornflakes tastes like dessert. I begin to discover cognates— such words as *banana*, *cereal*, and *coffee* that sound alike in English and Spanish, and have the same general meaning.

Zoraida pours thick, dark Cuban espresso into a white ceramic cup, adds steamed whole milk, and presents me with my first Cuban *café con leche*.

"Wow," I report to my father and Zoraida, who are both watching me. They smile and nod at each other knowingly.

"Do you normally eat cornflakes for breakfast?" I ask them.

"No," Zoraida says, scrubbing the spotless counter vigorously.

"We buy for you," my father adds.

I thank him even though I've probably eaten cornflakes only a handful of times in my entire life. My father goes to the pantry and gingerly pulls a macaroon from a plastic container. I love macaroons too, and he offers me one.

He narrates his past in a choppy present tense: "I work as psychiatrist twelve years in Baltimore State Hospital, Maryland." Even after twelve years, *Maryland*, on my father's tongue, remains "Mary"-land. Zoraida drops her dish towel on the counter, rubs her hands briskly over her upper arms as if she's shivering, and exclaims, "Cold!" My father charges his words with all the declarative force the present tense has to offer, as if he's giving dictation for a very important speech. I tilt my head and strain to catch every word. This first morning, everything feels present tense. Zoraida meticulously dusts the figurines in her china cabinet, burrowing the corner of her cotton cloth into the fold of every porcelain petticoat and collar. My father takes another macaroon from the tall, narrow cupboard in the kitchen, holds it aloft like he's proposing a toast, and eats it in two bites. A rim of sunlight glows from the Florida room around the corner. I take a sip of my coffee and decide there's nothing more present tense than café con leche. The thick, bitter espresso whipped into a frothy, sugary haze and folded into steamed whole milk momentarily pins the innate desire for sweet and bitter directly to the center of my being. Planted firmly on tall bamboo stools, my father and I are even sitting in the present tense. We are sitting at the same altitude, side-by-side for the first time, facing the same direction.

My father tells me he once met an English-speaking man who awoke from a long sleep and began to speak Spanish. The man, a patient in the institution in Maryland where he worked, had suffered a psychotic break and was heavily medicated. After a few days in a catatonic state, he regained consciousness.

"He say he hear Spanish until he is three years old, then no more. He say he know Spanish and like that, he speak it." My father tells me this, looking, as elderly people sometimes do, just a bit to the right of me and into the past where the story originally occurred. "And he do it," my father recounts, turning his attention back to me and Zoraida, who's only half listening as she pulls the burners from the electric stove and removes the metal pans beneath to scrub them.

I imagine a man with pallid skin stretched translucent over a hard, angular jawbone. Traces of that man protrude from his thick brow bone and prominent cheekbones. This man awoke in a land of metal mirrors. He heard the brisk rustle of support hose and skirts as nurses hurried past, the rattle of pens chained to clipboards, and finally, a colony of starched, white lab coats murmuring in Spanish. He too began to speak:

Habló en español lentamente. No era incertidumbre. Más bien, para cada cosa que se le ocurría (tengo sed, extraño a mi tío, quiero ver el color celeste)—encontraba forma y palabra. Habló lentamente por temor. Tenía miedo porque no sabía que hacer con está nueva lengua. Presentía que cada idioma, no se presenta limpio, preciso ni intacto como un regalo—se presenta como un parto, con dolor y con sangre y al construirse, destruye otras cosas.

"Suddenly, he stop. He become shy, and he stop," my father concludes. "Too much memories for psyche," he adds, tapping a forefinger to his temple with a clinician's certitude.

It must have been exhilarating for this patient to retrieve a part of himself long vanished, then suddenly, profoundly present. And how thrilling to temporarily usurp the world of the men in charge—these foreign doctors—to surprise and engage them on a level none of the other patients could. Still, the man retreated from Spanish. My father said that everyone was amazed and wanted to help the patient continue, but he refused. I think the man realized that a new language is not simply a trick of the tongue. Language demands everything of the speaker: breath, brain, saliva, and sweat—and it guarantees nothing in return. Even though he was recovering from a mental breakdown, traces of a healthy ego still existed. I believe my father's patient sensed the price a language exacts and responded with an appropriate measure of guardedness.

That morning, I grasp at my first words in Spanish, and my father exhilarates at my ability to recall words and pronounce them correctly after only one hearing. I navigate breakfast like a determined climber, hand-over-fist, clutching at cognates along the way:

plate/*plato*
cereal/*cereal*
banana/*banano*

My father is happy, and I'm thrilled. Zoraida looks at us cautiously, but with a trace of humor. I make my way to the bathroom and find my *toalla*. I am trembling, my knees buckling. I speak and push aside everything I've known. I put on my *pantalones y sandalias* and recognize *sofá*, *lámpara*, and *flores* for the first time. Hand-over-fist, the cognates bind me to my father like a strong nautical rope as the present tense unwinds before us. Questions and stories from the past would disrupt this delicate equilibrium. He says excitedly to Zoraida, "If she could be here for a whole summer, she'd be fluent." Zoraida looks skeptical, probably not about my capacity for language acquisition, but at the prospect of having me around for an entire summer.

That first day, *mi educación continúa con jamón* (my first Cuban sandwich) and the *carro* that takes us to the Librería Cervantes (which turns out to be a bookstore, not a library). My father buys me the book *Against All Hope*, the story of Armando Valladares, a political prisoner who was locked away in Cuba's notorious Isla de Pinos Prison for more than twenty years. My father follows me every step of the way, punctuating my words with, "Bien. Muy bien" and nodding to Zoraida with a look of approval. By lunchtime, I've cobbled together a remedial Spanish based on cognates and the meaning my imagination invents with each new word. *Por favor* is like asking for a favor and *gracias* is akin to saying grace.

I'll never know why my attempt to speak Spanish unearthed my father's memory of the catatonic man. Did he envision me as someone waking into a world of Spanish from a long English slumber? Did he think of me as having been infused with his language just because my mother once carried his seed?

I see us in the kitchen's artificial light. He's shuffling from one object to another, naming things, and I'm on his heels, enthusiastically repeating. It's like an Easter egg hunt, and I'm discovering chocolates at every turn, popping them in my mouth without restraint. I'm conjugating verbs and poring over a book about political prisoners. Even the man recently emerged from a catatonic state had the instinct to protect himself, not to launch headlong into a relationship that might require everything and give very little in return. But I don't. I cannot resist my father's attention and acceptance, and I'll do anything to hold on to it. It's as if today is my birthday and words are the cake. I dig my spoon into the center and scoop out the richest part before it's been sliced or served. I'm even willing to eat the flame. I'll risk burning my tongue to get to the sweetest part.

Zoraida

After lunch, my father takes his siesta and Zoraida retreats into the bright, cold Florida room on the other side of the house. I follow her, grabbing a magazine along the way in case I need to look engrossed in something, but before I can open it, she's flipped on the TV and is offering me an animated, detailed synopsis of her favorite *telenovela*. I try to match Zoraida's heavily accented analysis with the stricken expressions flashing across the screen, and it's surprisingly easy. Unbeknownst to either of them, *don* something or other, a mature, ruggedly handsome landowner, is the long-lost father of María, a pretty young brunette primly buttoned into a modest peasant skirt and blouse. I'm elated by the fact that I can actually understand the gist of a show in Spanish and relieved to find a connection, however trivial, with Zoraida. On a gut level, I know that if I am to have a relationship with my father, his wife must accept me, and I sense that her approval is not a given.

Unlike the dining room, with its large, solemnly polished oak table, and the living room, cushioned and sheathed in transparent plastic covers, the Florida room's rattan couch and swivel chairs are comfortably padded with overstuffed pillows in a jungle green, palm-leaf print. I relax into my chair and smile eagerly at Zoraida's chatter, the glucose of a Cuban lunch metabolizing into a sweet, drowsy haze.

When Zoraida talks about the telenovela, her voice shifts from its naturally brusque, declarative tone to the softer, hushed tones one might use to confide in someone. I can't completely follow the dizzying story line, but it's clear that she cares passionately about the fate of María and the don. She knows the intricate details of their lives—the clothes they've worn throughout the season, their hidden motives, and their secret food allergies—and reports all plotlines, major and minor, with a gossip columnist's passion for detail. María thinks her father died in a fire. I don't know what the don thinks, and when I attempt to ask Zoraida, she pauses with a confused look and changes the subject. "Oh, oh, this one, this lady," she points excitedly at an elegant elderly woman who enters the foyer of the mansion, "she sews beautifully."

Zoraida tells me that when she first left Cuba for the United States, she worked in a New Jersey coat factory as a seamstress. She waited several months for my father to join her. "My hand was so precise," she brags, "I got extra work sewing the bindings of rare books."

María is at the door. She's come looking for work and the gracious, older woman with the mane of silver hair coifed neatly into a bun directs her to a sitting area. María nods and smiles sweetly.

When it comes to her life, Zoraida reports the facts in brief, abrupt spurts. She never calls my father "José" or "husband." In her stories, he's always a pronoun. She tells me they had a long courtship in Cuba and that he was able to leave for the United States before she could, but even when she arrived, they didn't live together immediately: "I waited for *him*. Finally, *he* come and take me to Maryland where *he* work." She recounts this without taking her eyes off the TV.

María accidentally takes a wrong turn and stumbles into the don's office, where he's scrutinizing some important papers. Startled that she's interrupted the man of the house, she gasps. The don looks up. They share a meaningful, almost tender gaze, until María apologizes profusely and scurries off.

"Still, we not marry for long time," Zoraida continues, "He very stubborn, very particular," she adds raising a sharply arched eyebrow for emphasis. "One day, we walk by the courthouse," she throws her hands in the air in exasperation, "and he say, 'we marry!'"

In that one afternoon, I find out three important pieces of information: my father was in a supposedly committed relationship with Zoraida when I was conceived and born. I do the math. I'm sure Zoraida does the same math. I also discover that, for Zoraida, the news of my existence is recent. On the tail of her observation about my father's "particularity," she barks: "I know nothing about you until he tell me you're coming and to get ready the room." My face flushes hot with shame and shock. I'd wanted to know who my father was for so long, I'd never considered the possibility of having to justify or apologize for my presence. I look down at the back of the magazine in my lap. A confident, glossy Cover Girl face smiles back.

"I didn't know about 'me' until fairly recently either," I offer half-jokingly. A puzzled scowl flashes across Zoraida's thick, round face.

"What I mean to say is no one told me who my father was until I was sixteen," I clarify. "I thought he was dead." I'm careful not to mention my mother directly. With this information, Zoraida perks up and tells me she has a niece who had *un bebé ilegítimo*, or out of wedlock. "It's important for everyone to meet their father. It's natural," she declares. She doesn't say this with compassion or conviction. She says it as a fact of life—a hard bone one must bite down on when eating the meat. And with this, she reveals one more piece of information: she had always wanted children, but they couldn't conceive. She juts her chin toward the part of the house where my father's sleeping when she says "they." "My tests were fine," she adds sharply.

I've missed something. A shapely blonde wearing black jeans and a tight-fitting gold brocade jacket has discovered an unsettling letter in one of the drawers of the don's desk. The blonde shoots a look of malice at the camera, then stomps off as the credits start to roll. "Now it's going to be a big fight!" Zoraida says, flicking her wrist rapidly as if she had just scorched her finger on a pan. I'm lost. Who is the blonde? Don's young trophy wife? His "legitimate" daughter? I'm desperate to know, but I fear my questions are too obvious. Besides, Zoraida's already wiggling her chubby frame from her swivel chair. She leans over the TV to change the channel and launches into a breathless synopsis of another telenovela, this one set in colonial Brazil. Although nothing Zoraida says or does confirms it, the lead balloon sinking in my stomach tells me I've let down María in her most vulnerable moment and lost precious points with Zoraida.

While my mother was pregnant, my father was in a relationship with another woman who eventually became his wife. This woman knew nothing about my existence prior to my visit. My father and Zoraida were never able to have children, and she had assumed he was sterile. I tell myself these facts. I repeat them silently as I watch the Brazilian mouths just a fraction out of sync with the dubbed Spanish translation. I came all this way to meet my father. I'm here to fill in the gaps of my mother's fictions with truths, but what I'm hearing doesn't lend the coherence and sense of resolution I'd anticipated, and now before I can process this information, it begins to vanish. Soon, I will remember nothing. My memory is receding under this onslaught of information, emotions, and sensations. I vanish into the next telenovela and *arroz con leche*, an ice-cold dollop of vanilla sweetness with a pungent hint of lime.

In the end, I know nothing more about my father than I did before I met him. He remains a mystery. Who is he? Why didn't he have children with his wife? Why did he wait so long to marry her? Why didn't he ever look for me? In the meantime, I've caught a glimpse of my father and Miami. During this first trip to Miami, I begin to believe in the permanence and possibility of place. Places may change dramatically, but they rarely disappear. I know that people can hang up the phone, close the door, and return letters without opening them, but having barely left the state where I was born, I'm astonished by the democracy of travel. A city exists for everyone who chooses to enter it. So at twenty, I start to dream of travel in the same way many girls at that age dream of a lover. In my eyes, Miami is perfect: every star in Miami is the right star. Every mechanic is beautiful. Every cloud is benign.

Six years after visiting my father, I'll move to Miami. On the first day, I'll stand alone on the corner of 27th Avenue and US 1 and ask directions from an old man hawking *El Nuevo Herald*s from a stack of papers as high as his waist. I'll ask with my plain Midwestern accent, a slightly southern lilt in my vowels. I'll wear too many layers of clothing and speak too politely to be from Miami: "Pardon me, sir. Could you please point me in the direction of Coralway?" "Coral Way" will slide from my tongue in one big mouthful, the way I learned it from my father, with the *way* waxing toward a philosophical *why?* The man will look at me suspiciously and then smile, "Ahhh. You must have been in love with a Cuban who lived on Coral Way. You say it like a Cuban."

My father didn't give me explanations, apologies, or answers. He didn't "take responsibility" in any concrete way. He broke off language like pieces of hard candy that caught the light before dissolving in my mouth.

Manny, 1998

I hope and fear he'll ask me to dance.

He has a wide, luminous forehead and wavy, shoulder-length, brown hair pulled back in a ponytail. He stands close by while his friends chat with mine. When I excuse myself to go to the restroom, he steps aside, gallantly sweeping his arm outward. Juan Manuel, or Manny, as he calls himself, exaggerates every gesture because this is the only vocabulary we have. Mango's bamboo-covered bar, draped in a grass skirt, snakes through the large patio. Pairs of dancers grind to loud, throbbing salsa music. I speak enough Spanish to find out he came from Cuba a little more than a year ago. He works repairing air conditioners during the day and has aspirations of being a salsa singer. I turn my palm upward and pretend to be writing on it with the other hand.

"Secretaria?" he ventures.

"No!" I exclaim, more adamantly than I'd intended, and he jumps back with a puzzled look on his face. A friend yells over his shoulder without missing a beat of his own conversation:

"Escritora! Es escritora."

"Ahhh." he smiles broadly, his "ahhh" fading into silence as a brassy salsa trombone needles its long horn in and out of our non-conversation.

It's 1998. I moved to Miami a few years ago and spent the first two studying at the university, writing and reading, frustrated in the world of English and anxious to begin my life in Spanish. I attempt to ask Manny what he likes to do when he's not working, but he understands me to say, "Do you like your work?" and stretches his arms wide, hunching over as if under the weight of a large window unit. Just as I'm getting my syntax rearranged and ready to redeliver, one of the Mango's dancers, a voluptuous girl with a dark complexion and "Te amo Cali" printed across her chest, sashays by, curves her long manicured nails around Manny's forearm, and pulls him to the floor without looking at either of us. He'd mentioned that he might get a job dancing salsa and serving drinks. It looks like this is his audition.

At first, he's just playing around—chatting with "Te amo Cali," spinning her every now and then—but as the horns and percussion race forward with the urgency of a three-alarm fire, they start to move in a faster, more intricate pattern. He spins her then pivots on his heel and drops to the floor, bouncing up in the time it takes her to complete a turn. They cross wrists and turn inward, spinning continuously until their joined hands rise up and down like a butterfly's wings. In many ways, Manny looks like the typical *recién llegado*: pressed white jeans and a medallion of Nuestra Señora de la Caridad del Cobre (Cuba's patron saint) visible beneath the neck of his tight, short-sleeved T-shirt. Occasionally, he carefully touches his shirt or the waist of his jeans. He's not uncomfortable in his clothes, just aware of them, but when he dances, he is sensual and oblivious. His hips and forearms shift with a vibrancy closer to joy than showmanship, and an uninhibited spontaneity flutters around him like a colorful kite dangling from a child's wrist.

Everyone sitting around the bar turns to watch. Manny and his partner perform for the crowd now. I've noticed other couples slip in and out of awareness like that—one moment in a world of their own, the next extroverted and showing off before the audience. I envy it all— the intimacy, spontaneity, and audaciousness—as I watch Manny and his partner turn, dip, slide, and press into one another. The percussion beats faster until it overrides the song's melody and chorus. Manny shakes his body. Some women cheer as he stands behind his partner and lowers himself to the floor while his entire body continues to vibrate. Manny's musician friends sneer and joke amongst themselves. To them, he's a puppy tagging along because he's younger than they are and not a "real" musician (not trained in Cuba). All the while, he maintains his broad, good-natured smile. He even smiles my way a couple of times and sort of shrugs as if he himself has no idea how he's pulling off this feat of coordination and lower-body strength.

I hope and fear he'll ask me to dance. I know the guttural part, the instinctive, but I don't know the language of the four limbs. I don't know the steps. Salsa, like Spanish, is something I intuit and intone. Until recently, I was too proud to learn these things in the form of steps, chapters, and lessons. My friends are bored and head toward the door. Mango's is a place to have a salty margarita on a Sunday afternoon and either laugh at the spectacle or join in briefly and leave abruptly. The trumpet is waning and the song's chorus is winding down as the singer belts out one final tribute to his beloved's "ojitos bellos." Manny's on his feet and turning "Te amo Cali" in an obligatory fashion while they both scan the crowd. I know he's looking for me, not wanting me to think he has an interest in his dance partner. I make a dash for the exit and turn to wave goodbye at the last minute, so that he won't have time to follow.

Manny stands mute at my window, his white linen shirt flapping behind him. He's just been to New York to shop around his demo tape. He holds up his finger to indicate the number one, and when I ask if this was his first demo tape, he shakes his head no.

"First time on a plane?" I ask. He nods vigorously.

"How did you get to Miami then?"

He shrugs.

Soon, he'll be performing Tuesday and Thursday evenings at Mango's. He'll sing salsa over poorly recorded instrumentals with a Peruvian percussionist in the background. Between sets, he'll herd sunburned German tourists and businessmen from Milwaukee to their tables, smiling his gap-toothed smile and exclaiming, "Hola! I'm Manuel from Cuba." But for now he's Manny, aspiring recording artist. He unnecessarily ducks through the doorway when I invite him in. Removing a pillow covered in Indonesian batik and placing it carefully to the side as if it were a sleeping infant, he takes a seat. Manny is younger than I remember. He looks around my small studio apartment with interest, occasionally reverting his eyes to the ground. Late-afternoon sunlight fills my apartment. This combined with the rush of water from the fountain outside make Manny's white clothes almost blinding. I can hardly look at him.

We try to communicate, and my limited Spanish allows for a basic exchange, but whenever he starts to take off, the velocity of his words loses me—a trip he took (where?), someone who was going to help him record a better-quality demo tape. (Or did that happen already?) There's not enough language between us to fill the awkward silence. All we have is ourselves, and our attraction sits before us like an ostentatious present that we don't know how to open.

He takes his wallet from his pants pocket and pulls out a creased photo of his mother and sister back in Cuba. The sister is very light-skinned. His mother's skin has a dark, burnt sienna tone. Manny is somewhere in between.

"And your father?" I ask.

"French," he enunciates carefully in English.

I start to ask if he knew him, but he cuts me off, shaking his head no, and returns the question by jutting his chin toward me.

I've been conjugating the two verbs, *saber* and *conocer*. They both mean "to know," and I try to squeeze my thoughts into the correct one:

"Mi papá," I venture, "No lo conozco."

Conocer. The verb hangs in the air like the steel blade of a guillotine. *Conocer* means to meet and to know. Yes, I've met him, but no, I don't know him. How do I join the meeting and the not knowing of my father in one verb? It's more than a grammatical question.

Manny raises his eyebrows, somewhat surprised by my statement, perhaps confused, but quickly reverts to his former friendly self. I imagine his father, an idealistic French backpacker enamored with socialism wandering through Old Havana in the late seventies and meeting up with a beautiful *mulata* from the neighborhood. I imagine my mother, a thirty-three-year-old widowed nurse who lives with her parents, smitten with my father, a tall, light-eyed Cuban sent to Louisville, Kentucky, to recertify his license to practice medicine in the United States. Manny and I are by-products of such unlikely unions. Neither planned nor orphaned, we haven't been recognized either.

In 1989, my grandmother dies. My mother and I make arrangements over the phone to meet in Louisville for the funeral. Before hanging up, she hesitates then tells me that most of the family and friends who will attend the funeral "don't know about me."

"What do you mean?" I ask.

"They don't know you were born." I knew I didn't exist for my father and his family, but I had no idea that besides my mother's parents and her sister, most of her relatives didn't know I'd been born.

I attend the traditional, no-frills Southern funeral: white lilies and black stockings. The organ groans a somber version of "Just As I Am." I stand near a tarnished silver coffeepot and survey the expanse of white-haired second and third cousins wandering like sleepwalkers in and out of the labyrinth of cushioned parlors. My hair is pulled tightly into a French braid, an indestructible fortress of bobby pins and tortoiseshell combs lacquered into place with enough Aqua Net to hold for the next few days of viewing, singing, and praying.

My mother appears and squeezes my arm as if we've just run into each other at a cocktail party. "We're really getting through this quite well," she says under her breath, without letting any crack show in her wide, impenetrable smile. It's too late to say I'm still reeling from finding out so many people don't even know I exist. We've sped ahead to the part where everyone meets me, and on the surface at least, "approves." I'm spinning in a cocoon that I'll later identify as anger.

Manny seems so nonchalant. I wonder what he thinks of his father, the invisible Frenchman who fucked his mother then took off, leaving his *liberté*, *égalité*, and *fraternité* spinning between her ears and his seed firmly planted in her belly. I take Manny's hands in mine, pull him to standing, and lead him toward the corner of the room away from the large window facing the street. This quiet moment seems like a good time to share my secret—that despite all logic, I'm convinced that if I can learn to dance, my father's absence won't be such a painful fact.

"Show me how to dance." I say in English. Manny smiles. He walks over to a CD player sitting on a small metal table. He's not going to find any salsa in my collection of Chopin, Billie Holiday, and Patsy Cline. I signal to him, "No, nothing there." He flips on the radio, and static spews out. He doesn't bother to turn down the volume before he starts fiddling with the dial. Dance music and commercials in Spanish erupt in crass, sputtering blips that bounce from my hardwood floors to the barren stucco walls, making me feel as if I'm in a tin can. All of a sudden, everything feels wrong. I don't want to lodge myself between Manny and the horns of some flashy, overproduced salsa as if my apartment were an annex to Mango's.

I walk over and touch the top of his head. He looks up earnestly as if he's changing a flat. I nod at the radio and shake my head no. He turns it off, and I pull him by his hand back to the corner. I feel flushed. I'm not sure what I want, but I know that it must happen in silence. Even music would interrupt the dance I want to learn. Manny walks behind me, and I tense up. He puts his hands on my hips and pulls me close. He's not a huge man, but his hands are large. He starts to make a clucking sound with his tongue on the roof of his mouth: one, two. Pause. One, two, three. I've heard farmers herd cattle and horses to a similar sound, but Manny's version is more rhythmic than repetitive. He starts to step right then left. I follow.

"Criollita," he whispers in my ear. I hold in a surprised breath. It's a word I hear frequently, but never so close to my ear, never in a voice bordering on serious. Cuban construction workers yell it from atop buildings, sometimes even throwing in a "Hail Mary!" My friends' Cuban boyfriends always greet me with a playful elbow or peck on the cheek.

"What's up, Criollita?" they ask, the word *Criollita* springing from their lips as if they're radio hosts introducing me as the next hit song. Later, when I can speak Spanish, Cuban women I meet casually (shopping clerks, manicurists, dressing room attendants) will confide: "Muchacha, you have the perfect cuerpo de criollita." It will be some time before I understand what this really means, but for now I know it has to do with the part of me I've been trying to cover up since adolescence—my backside. Manny keeps time, and I place my hands on his: *un, dos* (pause) *un, dos, tres.*

In the middle of a vast field on the edge of a housing development in Missouri, I'd prepared for this moment. Like any girl on the brink of adolescence, I knew intuitively that I would soon go out into the world and my body would join in conversations with others. I'd enter the swaying and spinning. I'd step into the embraces, turns, and dips, but first, I was compelled to dance without a partner or music. Like any teenager, I wanted to move and to watch myself move without the conspiracy of another's arms, legs, and hips. That summer before my sixteenth birthday, cement slabs had been poured and across from our two-room duplex, dozens of barren basements waited to be topped with ranch-style and split-level family homes. I lived in the hallway, in front of the only full-length mirror in the apartment. I was the wreath spray-painted gold and wrapped around the frame. I stared at my dancing form and danced before my own fixed eyes. My narrow shoulders, small, firm breasts, and thin, tapered waist were winding toward a mystery that would take years to unravel: the story of my two bodies. Peering from the mirror, I grew transparent in the conversion of my thighs from solid flesh to the humming.

I shift my weight in time with Manny's clucking tongue, rhythmic lower body, and almost inaudible humming. Neither anticipating nor imitating his movements, I circle my hips beneath his hands. He starts to interject a verse here and there in a raspy, almost absentminded voice. I tuck my hips inside his. Without music or sound, we move faster and faster, toward the *timba*, the part of the salsa where the percussion overrides the song's chorus, melody, and even rhythm. It's exhilarating to let one section of my body chatter so wildly to the world. Finally, we fall to the floor in a laughing, sweaty, playful heap. He clutches his chest and gasps for air dramatically, then gives me the thumbs up. Manny, beautiful, childlike. He touches my face. I'm nervous. The courtship stage has sped past us. A small-town voice surfaces to my consciousness and chides, "Boys who don't take you to a movie or stand in line at the keg to get you a beer only want one thing." Manny keeps wiping his hands on his white shirt as if there's something on them. Isn't that what we both want? That one thing?

"Why are you wearing white?" I ask.

"Initiation," he smiles shyly and touches a warm hand to my face.

"Who is your santo?"

"Elegguá."

"Look," I volunteer, "I have an Elegguá candle." I take the tall, white candle ensconced in glass from the shelf, peel off the gummy Publix sticker, and read: "Elegguá: Messenger of the other gods, protector of the home, saint of crossroads." I burn my candle and pray a little. Manny smiles. I smile.

He holds a condom up to the light. We watch the liquid swirl around, and I imagine animated creatures with tadpole-like tails swishing about and swimming in circles within the sagging sheath. Although he's only twenty-three, Manny has a six-year-old son, and he's still marveling at how he made him. We drift for a while on my bed, a raw wooden frame with a thin Japanese mattress unrolled across the top. I marvel at the fact that even with the language barrier, I've managed to find Manny. It seems I have a sixth sense for fatherless men.

Joshua's parents had slept in separate rooms as long as he could remember. His father kept a lock on his door and would go for weeks, sometimes months, without saying a word to him or his brothers. Jaime was raised by Jesuits. Daniel overheard he didn't have the same father as his siblings at a family reunion. These are the arms in which I've felt most comfortable. These men don't ask about my family because they don't want to discuss theirs. With others, "Where are your parents from?" comes up immediately. It's spoken before the waiter brings the bread, before the clutch is shifted to fourth gear.

I elbow Manny and joke, "What do you have that's French?" He shrugs and a smile flashes across his face, but his forehead darkens slightly when he says the word "nothing." His left thigh is flung across my abdomen and stretches the width of the mattress. He takes my hand and places it between his legs, beneath the darkest part. The thin, cool flesh presses into my palm. We're staring at the ceiling. The English word *ceiling* comes from the Latin *caelum*, or "constellation," and has the same root as the Spanish word *cielo*. *Cielo* can mean either heaven or sky. Which one is Manny staring at? Manny's father is out there somewhere. The man with whom he shares his blood, bone, and pigment is moving through the world, washing himself, buying a ticket for something, tearing off a piece of bread.

It's dusk now and the flicker of the candle in the kitchen illuminates nothing. So little light only creates shadows and the illusion of movement. In the darkness, a wave emerges and subsides with each breath. It ripples through my wrist to my shoulder and upper back until I feel as if I am floating. This must be what it's like to be on a raft at sea. With the bobbing of the waves, the movement must be more vertical than horizontal and very quickly the question becomes not "Will I make it?" but rather "Have I left or arrived?" At what point, after uncounted hours at sea, does one shift from being a person on a journey to a piece of flesh, a row of vertebrae pressed into the slab of wood hovering between el cielo and the ocean floor?

I've read that in the summer of 1994 more than 30,000 Cubans left the island in homemade rafts. Since then, more than 150,000 have made the journey, and thousands more have drowned trying. From so many thousands, one has washed ashore and lies beside me. I feel Manny's other life enter the room now. He sits up, scoots to the edge of the wooden frame, and although he closes his eyes, pressing his forehead to the backs of my hands in a gesture I know to mean "I will return," I know he won't. He has somewhere else to be, somewhere he was supposed to be hours ago. I feel it now, and for the first time Manny looks tired and weary. The shadow of the Elegguá candle flickers from the kitchen like someone shuffling around, preparing coffee. He lies back down for a few more seconds and stares at the ceiling, worried no doubt about the little boy, the job repairing air conditioners, and who knows what else. His chest rises and falls quickly and lightly like an old man's. It occurs to me that maybe Manny lost someone on that raft. Maybe someone lying next to him, almost sharing his same breath, slid into the dark waters, uncoiled like a rope, and vanished.

He sits up again, and this time plows ahead in his departure. I ask him to bring me a can of 7Up when he returns. My stomach is queasy and 7Up always comforts me. He nods his head vigorously, and even though I'm convinced he won't return, that he'll never return, I can't help but look out the window well after he's gone. As my soup is heating up and I start to sort laundry for washing, I look down at the spot where Manny stood in his white clothes, his forehead wide and luminous. From the corner of my eye, I catch a glimpse of the thin mattress and rickety wooden frame. Here, we told father stories while trumpets, congas, and cowbells pulsated between the walls. Here, there was touching and biting and laughing. Here, the clothes untangled themselves from our limbs. Now, there is nothing.

I marvel at the nothingness of the room. The doors closed like shut eyes. A portable CD player on a metal table, a simple mattress and frame, silent piles of clothing, permanence, dissolution, flame, and wave—my father's hands finding mine for the first time at the airport. As we walk away, I look over my shoulder and the spot where we stood has already vanished and reappeared as the site of more reunions and goodbyes. The stiff black coats of Hasidic Jews and the bulging rainbow-colored knit cap of a Rasta fill the space where we just stood. I watch as families around me wave frantically at suitcase-laden passengers disembarking. My father is ahead, now shuffling under the weight of my bag. His wife's farther ahead, her stark profile flashing left then right. I try to hold on to my father's English, which is quickly sinking beneath a clucking, rolling, trilling tide of Spanish. He looks back to see that I'm there. His face flushes a smile and his Cuban mouth tears off a piece of English like a dry hard roll.

"Something stars," he blurts out.

"Stars? Huh?" I cock my head and squint my eyes upward, trying to get a glimpse of stars on the ceiling of the Miami International Airport. Seeing me, my father shouts over his shoulder, "Tú. Eres una estrella." He's leveled his Spanish so clearly and emphatically my way that even I understand. It's me. I'm the star he's pointing toward. I'm the rush of color to his pallid face. At that moment, I want nothing more than to belong to the tribe that speaks my father's tongue.

Manny does return. His white clothes make their appearance in front of the fountain outside my window. I tell him I'm going to be traveling soon, without saying where; he gives me a smile of recognition. Manny writes me a little note in Spanish: "Every journey must begin and end with Eleggguá. Only he can obstruct and open paths."

In 1998, although Cuban Americans are allowed visas, no one in Miami talks openly about going to Cuba. Thousands of Cuban Americans go every year, but they don't broadcast it to their neighbors. They buy large, cheap, canvas duffel bags from the Pakistanis in downtown Miami. In the line at Sam's Club or Navarro, they may catch a glimpse of one another over heaps of ballpoint pens, jumbo-sized packets of vitamins, and super-absorbent tampons, but no one speaks.

Who knows which neighbor will be the one to shout out "Comunista!" making one an outcast at the corner cafeteria or forever ruining any chance of a promotion at Dade County Water and Sewer? While I don't live within this community of exiles and I'm not obliged to justify my actions to them, the shroud of disapproval and even animosity that hangs over the mere mention of travel to Cuba is so palpable I make my plans in silence. As an American, I'm forbidden to travel to Cuba. It's illegal. As a Cuban American, I'm illegitimate. I've never seen my birth certificate or any other official form that identifies my parents. To the U.S. government, my Y chromosome is pure fiction. My lineage, my birthright, consists of a palm-sized photo of my father I've seen only a few times, a couple of muddled stories, and a visit to Miami when I was twenty. I imagine trying to explain this to some overweight, bored Cuban American bureaucrat at the Office of Immigration and Naturalization on Biscayne and 79th Street. "Now who is your father again?" she might ask, rolling her eyes, little flakes of guava pastry dangling from her upper lip as she enunciates "who?"

I've answered that question once before. That *pregunta* question, that telenovela question, that accusatory question. I was eighteen. Two years after my mother told me my father was alive, I asked her for a way to contact him. From a drawer overflowing with papers she produced the only contact information she had: the address of his brother, Eduardo Alsina, in Chicago. I sealed some photos of myself and a letter inside an envelope and placed that in a larger envelope with a request that Eduardo forward it to my father. I never received either a response or a "return to sender."

Two years later, when I was a sophomore in college, a roommate persuaded me to call. I'd kept the contact information on a scrap of paper in my address book for two years, never writing it in or throwing it away. I'd thought of calling so many times, but on this day over diet Cokes and Marlboro Lights, my peppy roommate, Mary McMullin, chirps something cliché like, "You'll never know if you don't try" and I think I can do it. I can just pick up the phone, dial my father's brother in Chicago, and ask for my father's address. I go into the other room. The air-conditioning unit rattles. I untangle the cord and pull the phone as far from the door as possible. The bedside table is cluttered with an overflowing ashtray, tubes of hair gel, and rolls of Lifesavers candies, but for one moment I don't smoke, swallow, or even breathe. I dial. A woman answers "Hello?" with a foreign accent.

"May I speak with Eduardo, please?"

"Who is this?" The voice at the other end sounds cold, almost defensive.

"Who is this?" the woman repeats.

Finally, I blurt out, "I'm José's daughter" and it's as if I've answered "Matthew, Mark, Luke, or John," disciples no one believed in the first place, dead fish for hands, seaweed in their hair, stars falling from their beards.

The phone slams down in my ear.

Ironically, this call was the impetus for my first meeting with my father. A few months later, when we finally met, he told me that his brother and sister-in-law had opened the envelope of photos out of curiosity and hid them from him out of shame. My spontaneous call scared them into telling him the truth. That phone slamming in my ear ultimately connected us, but it also startled me toward a new reality. For the first time, I felt the danger, the potentially irreversible pain that might come from meeting my father or anyone close to him. I also realized that I'd unconsciously viewed myself as the victim. I'd thought of myself as the person who deserved an explanation or an apology, but that defensive voice on the other end of the phone line revealed a reality I'd never considered: I might be someone to avoid. I could be an intruder or troublemaker best kept at bay.

Soon, I will go to Bogotá, Colombia. The Spanish I know and don't know will unfurl from my tongue. I have a chance to teach writing at Javeriana University. This is the only way I'll learn—immersion. I'll put my things in storage and convert my broken Spanish into full sentences, paragraphs even. Then I'll work, exchanging pesos for dollars, to go to Cuba. I fantasize about coming back and speaking to Manny. I imagine myself returning to Miami, fluent in all the steps and conjugations and dancing with him. Preparing to leave, I dream of speaking to him, but with each new border, I forget him. With each new mouthful of language, he becomes not a destiny, but one more rock on a rocky path.

El Goce Pagano

Bogotá. Men and women dart across busy streets with handkerchiefs pressed to their mouths. Street workers wear surgical masks. Clouds of black smoke roll from ailing busses and minivans. The sky matches the wet asphalt as I ride to and from my job at the Javeriana, a Catholic University where I teach English.

Language is what led me here, and now that I've arrived, I'm amazed at how much and how little Spanish I possess. I walk, take the bus, and buy groceries—all in Spanish. Yet I ask questions using the wrong pronoun; speak of the past in the present; and most crucially, try to speak of my needs, doubts, and hopes without the subjunctive. Rarely used in English, the subjunctive suffuses Spanish. For now, my desires are crudely chopped into childlike declarations. Not, "I hope we will eat soon," but "I want food." I scrunch my knees to my chest on the crowded, green microbus filled with twangy Vallenato music that takes me to and from the Javeriana. I teach English, learn Spanish, earn pesos, buy dollars—all in anticipation of a trip I'll make. I still believe that travel is a democratic right, even though my father happens to be from the only country in the Western Hemisphere off-limits to me. Colombia seems like the next best alternative.

A friend from Miami has broken off with her boyfriend and comes to visit Bogotá "for a change of pace." We pull up to a gray, rectangular slab of concrete called El Goce Pagano, a small bar in downtown Bogotá frequented by students, activists, and intellectuals from La Nacional, Bogotá's state-run, left-leaning university. In a city wracked with political conflict, El Goce Pagano has survived decades of bomb threats and impromptu closings. A long, narrow window stretches the length of the building. Breath, sweat, steam, and smoke churn out of the window's thin iron slats. Inside, the walls are surprisingly cold and clammy, while the packed center of the dance floor radiates a smoldering, patchouli-scented vapor. We check our coats behind the bar and rush to the dance floor. I'm anxious to unwind with my friend after several weeks of immersion in the formalities and euphemisms of Bogotá's middle-class culture, so I push my way to the floor, where people dance in trios, couples, small groups, and alone. Traditional *son cubano* and African spirituals spin around us from crackling vinyl records. This isn't the overproduced salsa of Miami. It's Cuba, really Cuba, and for the first time, it feels like a separate entity from Miami. Cuba is no longer a place I've heard about. It's a place that exists despite what I've heard. The reality of the choices I've made starts to sink in. I've temporarily rearranged my life so that I can go to Cuba.

After several songs, we take a break and go to the bar. I sip an *aguardiente* on ice and observe the skinny, middle-class Colombian kids dressed in brightly colored ponchos and hand-woven textiles typically worn by the indigenous population. They bum cigarettes, talk politics, and rub their bony hips together as they dance. A *son* about Changó comes on. I know from my friends in Miami that in the Afro-Cuban religion Santería Changó is the god of war and drums, the macho of all machos. My friend and I recognize the slow, heavily syncopated rhythm, and we race to the dance floor. We dance side by side, crossing the left foot over the right and making a small dark square, a sort of box step with rhythm. This is the line dance for Changó that we learned once at a party.

A short guy with closely cropped hair comes up beaming and starts to dance with us. He steps between us and falls into the rhythm of the dance, playfully stumbling over his own steps. He introduces himself as Alejandro, and as soon as I hear his Spanish, I know he's Cuban. People are shouting and cheering as the DJ switches the mood and starts spinning Colombian *cumbia*. I lean close to Alejandro and shout, "Cubano?" When I step back to see his response, he nods enthusiastically, and my friend and I shout over the music that we're from Miami.

"Ahh," his face lights up.

"Have you been there?" I ask, realizing my question could come across as a joke or insult, depending on Alejandro's political leanings.

We lean in to hear him say he's never had the opportunity to visit "that part of the world," but he's very curious about it. A wave of clove cigarettes and hashish wafts through the crowd. The three of us look at the gyrating cumbia dancers shouting "Huepa!" and we break into laughter. In this way, I meet Alejandro, a Cuban philosopher attending an anti-globalization conference in Bogotá. Turning the sharp corners of Changó's drum, somewhere between Havana and Miami, we meet and immediately embrace the irony: despite the fact that he's never been to Miami and I've never visited Havana, a friendly familiarity percolates between us.

When he smiles, Alejandro's face and throat reveal a few creases, exuding something canine and trustworthy. We dance to a few more songs until El Goce Pagano shuts down for the night. As people gather up their belongings, talk circulates of an after party at a Spanish tavern nearby. We invite Alejandro along.

The small brick building with a heavy wooden door appears sealed shut, but the taxi driver assures us it's open and drives off. In Bogotá, bars must close at 1:00 a.m. in order to curb violence. Clandestine after-hours clubs such as this one have sprung up in response. After a few minutes of knocking and waiting, the door opens and we're quickly ushered inside. The place is bustling. As my eyes adjust to the light, I recognize many of the same faces from the Goce Pagano. There's a large fireplace with a stone hearth in the center of the space. Moorish candelabras and swords hang on the walls. Alejandro guides us through the crowd and finds a small table. The song "Son de la Loma" comes on, and I ask if he's familiar with it. I don't know if the Cuban government plays much prerevolutionary music on the radio.

"Of course," he smiles shyly. "But it's been a long time. It's nice to hear." Beyond that, we hardly speak. Freed from the Goce Pagano's clammy shadows, we steal sidelong glimpses of each other. Alejandro's honey-colored skin defies black or white. He has a broad nose, finely drawn lips, and brown-gray eyes. My friend is dancing, chatting, and accepting drinks. The more Alejandro and I listen to the music, the more silent we become. The clear, crisp, rhythm of the *clave* and the *sonero*'s melancholic voice urge me to rise out of my chair and move my hips. I can see Alejandro wants to ask me to dance. He turns to me a couple of times and even starts to extend his hand, but I pretend to be looking intently at something in another direction or I ask him a question that requires more than a yes or no answer.

"Why do they keep singing about going to the *monte*?"

Alejandro tells me the same thing that fueled the Cuban Revolution also fueled *el son*: hunger. The revolution of 1959 did not blaze a path into Havana. It followed a path already well worn by starving farmers who came from the provinces looking for food. Cane harvesters, tobacco farmers, and shoemakers formed the first septets and trios in the early thirties. Decades later, the same unsteady hooves and swaggering mules carried fighters down from *la sierra* into Havana to oust Batista. I listen closely for some kind of pro-Castro rhetoric, for some Viva la Revolución hype embedded in this little bit of history, but Alejandro is soft-spoken and quietly passionate. He enunciates *hunger* and *farmer* slowly and carefully as if he reveres the words, yet *revolución* has the efficient, dull ring of a car part. Still, just hearing the word *revolución* spoken as a fact of history instead of a curse is jarring.

The people milling around begin to meld into dancing couples. One tall, lanky man clutches his partner and pulls her into his chest fiercely. His pelvis tilts toward her and his angular arms and elbows surround her petite, voluptuous shape like the wooden frame of a house. Others are dancing for measure, timing each turn perfectly, synchronizing cross-steps with precision and showmanship.

I tell Alejandro my father was Cuban. He looks surprised then pleased. Before he can respond, I add, "Well, I haven't seen him in a long time, but I suppose he's still Cuban." He leans forward with a per-plexed wrinkle across his brow and forehead, but before I can come up with another way of phrasing it, his face lights up and he laughs. "Once a Cuban always a Cuban—that's our curse." It's strange to just put the fact out there, after so many years of shaping conversations to avoid identifying my father.

"His last name is Alsina," I volunteer. He pauses to consider, then says he's heard the name but doesn't know any Alsinas. *Calma, calma,* I tell myself. I feel dizzy, overly anxious, and I can see Alejandro's chest lift then collapse as he lets out one big exhalation.

Finally, he raises his eyebrows, rubs his temples, and asks: "Why do I feel so nervous?" He runs his hand over his closely cropped black and gray hair, exhales again audibly, and laughs at himself. "It's you. You're making me nervous," he declares.

"Me?" I say, relieved that I don't have to admit my own anxiety. He nods and smiles jubilantly as if he's pleasantly surprised to find some-one's made him nervous.

"Is it because you see me as the enemy?" I ask half-jokingly. Alejandro cocks his head and smiles quizzically.

"I mean, if you see me as someone of Cuban descent from Miami, you think Miami mafia, Cuban right-wingers, and so on, right?" I have no idea where I'm going with this. I can feel a huge smile hardening on my face, "Or if you see me as an American, I'm a Yankee. Yanqui, right?

That's what they say in Cuba, right? In Colombia, they say gringo, but that actually originated in Mexico. . . ." I can hear myself babbling, hanging myself on the long rope of injustices the United States has committed against Latin America, and I want more than anything to shut up, but I can't find a stopping place in this diatribe.

Alejandro looks amused and says, "Let's dance." He waits for me to stand first, and we make our way to the "dance floor," a space only a few feet away where several tables have been pushed aside. All around us people are peeling off jackets and heading to the dance floor, shouting out drink orders and drumming their hands on the tables. Alejandro looks at me expectantly. I don't want this to be the first time. I don't want to look like a beginner. I want to be sure-footed, well versed in the language of dance, fluent in the turns and steps. But I'm bound to stumble. Hearing my father's last name in Alejandro's mouth, I feel less connected to it than ever. *Alsina.* The name rings as clinical and objective as a tree's genus and species: my family tree.

"Martínez, Fernández, Rodríguez," my mother hesitated and continued in a flourish of her regal script. "Rodríguez, José. Fernández, Eduardo." Fourth grade. In the school parking lot on personal heritage day, my mother forged my family tree. I remember asking, "But if he's dead, don't you have something written somewhere with the real names?" She looked up with her eyes brimming, threatening to drown us both in tears. I paused and dutifully formed the picture I always erected in my imagination for these rare moments when we mentioned my father. I saw him in a long, severe, immaculately polished mahogany coffin that stood too isolated to be in an actual funeral. He was a dark man, with hair darker than well water, slicked back. It was a glimpse of a funeral one might see on TV, a box within a box, neither one containing anything real-life. Moments like these were evidence of what I'd always sensed—that none of it was true.

I turn to Alejandro apologetically, "I really don't know what I'm doing."

"You do. *Sabes*," he emphasizes, and because in Spanish the verb conveniently pockets the pronoun, they coexist in one word and somehow sound more resolute. "You're a beautiful dancer. A natural," he smiles. He puts his hand on my waist. By American standards, Alejandro is short, but I've always liked men close to my height. I've never wanted to be towered over or engulfed. I remember my mother saying, "Put yourself so close to your partner, you're not following his dancing, you're following how he listens to the music." I resolve not to care about doing it right or wrong. I resolve to do as my mother said and just try to listen to the music as he listens to it. Not following exactly, but yes, following. We stop sitting between songs and instead stand like two kids, eager to hear what they'll put on next. He spins me around. He turns me before the chorus, creating a counterpoint, interjecting another opinion to the call-and-response of the song. One thing I'm a natural at—*las vueltas.* I can spin in circles endlessly without growing dizzy. I embrace the turns, the headiness, the trance of it like a Sufi practitioner whirling into a state of ecstasy.

Alejandro and I coil and recoil into consecutive turns and spins without letting go of each other. We clasp hands, raise our arms, and spin under the bridge of our wrists. I think to myself that later on, someday, I will tell him what I really wanted to say when I was blathering on, spewing out my secondhand information about the Miami mafia and right-wing exiles. I will tell him that, in fact, I know only one exile—my father, José Ignacio Alsina—whom I met when I was twenty and he was seventy-three, whose wife thought he was sterile until I appeared, making an already unhappy marriage nearly unbearable. I'll tell him I met José Ignacio Alsina with great hopes of getting to know my roots, of having a relationship with the man who claimed I was his only child, but that after that first visit, I never got through again. I'll tell Alejandro that in fact I'm not the daughter of an exile, but the exile of an exile. All of this I will tell Alejandro, when I find the words to say it in Spanish, when I find the words to say it to myself.

We dance until we're soaked with sweat. I think the *son* is a four-legged animal. It's music to be mounted, ridden, and traveled upon. We drink water and dance. As with any burro, mule, or horse and its rider, a small space exists between the *son* and the couple being carried by it. We fill carafes, bottles, plastic cups, and wine glasses with water until the pouring water echoes the rain on the cobblestones outside and on the aluminum roof above our heads. The *son* uses the four legs of its dancers to transport itself. In that way, I make my first trip to Cuba with Alejandro on a makeshift dance floor in a small Spanish tavern in Bogotá, Colombia. Our feet throb. Our faces glisten. In the small zone between the worn-down heels of my scuffed black shoes and the multicolored wool sweater someone lent Alejandro for the cold, all travel is possible. We dance until the owner is calling his wife from the back of the kitchen to help place the chairs on top of the tables and mop down the floor and my friend is laughing at us from the back of the room as she fans herself and fends off last-minute invitations.

In the *son*, there's a movement from the melodic to the rhythmic and percussive, from the straight back and long neck to the undulating hips. Our dancing follows this course, but my emotions run the other way. As the spinning slows down and the turns diminish, I start to feel melancholic and withdrawn. Musicians describe the phenomenon of meeting up, playing for hours, and then going their separate ways without having exchanged more than a few words. Is this what will happen with Alejandro tonight? I've never danced with someone for so long. We dance beyond the allotted time and wait between songs, our hands clasped like anxious children. What does it mean to place my hand on Alejandro's shoulder and let him send barely perceptible pulses to the insides of my knees and my palms? What does it mean for Alejandro to bend me backward, plunging me head-first into the dips and lunges of my parents' generation? For me, dancing that first night with Alejandro means wanting to let someone close to me—not for pleasure, but for something closer to joy.

The cab driver stops at a cold, quiet building on a hill. Alejandro sits in the front seat, and my friend and I are in the back. He's already written out his contact information in handsome, slightly curved letters. Later, I'll examine the card—Alejandro's last name and Cuba's ominous .cu extension in his e-mail address. Alejandro starts to say something, sees his breath hanging in the chilly air, and smiles shyly. He pulls a few Colombian pesos from his jacket and counts them gingerly. A one-dollar bill surfaces among the pesos. He pauses, carefully folds the bill, and puts it in another pocket. There's something absurd about seeing George Washington's alabaster forehead and ruffled shirt materialize in Alejandro's hand. How many hands has George passed through to make it to this taxicab in the Candelaria section of Bogotá, Colombia, where a man from a fishing village in Cuba and a woman from a town in rural Missouri want to kiss goodnight? It's a fairly recent policy change that dollar bills are legal in Cuba. Not so long ago, people were jailed for possessing them. Leave it to George Washington to appear at this moment and represent the power-wielding currency of my country.

Alejandro pays the cab driver and pauses. He quickly takes my face between his hands and kisses me on the forehead. Alejandro's eyes are like those of an infant whose eye color is yet to be established, an uncertain brown. A slight gray ring hovers at the rim of his iris when the headlights from a passing car flash across his face. Alejandro's eyes still haven't decided on their color.

I wake up touching myself. I'm curled on my side, my forehead bent in concentration. Then I'm open. I press the soles of my feet together. The insides of my thighs shudder and I hear waves. Is it the rustle of sheets or the rush of blood? This morning every movement heaves its weight toward a rock and a shore. I'm getting closer to Cuba, which means I'm getting closer to the sea, so I prepare for solitude with white candles and small bodies of water—baths of eucalyptus and salts, lilacs floating in mineral water.

After a long bath, I get dressed and step out of the damp, gray alcove of my apartment into the damp, gray alcove of Bogotá. I walk a few blocks to order *un caldo de res*, a deep abiding broth at the center of cold Andean Sundays. After several hours of being cloaked in Alejandro's informal Cuban *tú*, the Colombian *usted* rings hollow and false. As I watch people passing by, energy drains from my body. I'm tired of taking green buses that lurch and crawl past gray buildings constructed of cold, soot-colored stones—I'm tired of being passed by and of passing by others—hordes of people embalmed in gray clothing—all buttoned up, scarved, gloved, and hatted.

My soup arrives. I wrap my hands around the steaming bowl, an entire city at the edge of my table. Someone snapped bones and skinned off the meat for this soup. Hands, now absent, chopped off the gritty tops of carrots and rooted out the potato's bitter eyes. They pinched parsley and cilantro from their stems. Perhaps the hands sulked at the body's sides or hurried to perform other tasks while the broth followed the trajectory of a heated discussion—a rolling boil then a rapid simmer that steeps into a placid surface.

In the center of the restaurant, three tables are pushed together and lined with a family of men—three boys, a baby, two fathers, and a grandfather—all with close-set eyes and long, handsome, equine faces. The two eldest boys play jacks at the end of the table. The grandfather of this clan wears a simple but perfectly fitting gray suit coat and a black felt hat with a wide brim pushed back over a gleaming, sunburned forehead. The old man lifts a gray glistening thigh bone from his soup, holds it up in an archaic gesture, and places it on a white platter of fat and gristle. He squeezes a wedge of lime into the broth methodically. A waiter and a waitress bring platters of roasted potatoes and chicken. There are men who don't sit at tables. They preside. Is it deep-seated dignity or profound hypocrisy, this rod bolted down the backs of men who sit at tables like kings?

The first night I met my father, he called to me from his study where he sat imperious behind a great oak desk. In twenty years he had never called for me, tried to look for me, or even sent my mother a penny; yet somehow he looked complacent, authoritative even. I perched in the chair, hugging my knees to my chest, expectant and dizzy. He pulled out his wallet, and a creased baby photo (the only one my mother ever sent him) emerged from a crevice behind the plastic window that held his driver's license. He looked from me to the picture and asked, "What took you so long to find me?" This was not a sentimental moment. My father did not plan on having me, nor did he want to participate in my upbringing. He had not spent years looking for me. He came from Cuba at age fifty. For twenty years, he trained and worked as a doctor in the United States. He married and finally retired—all of this without telling his wife about me. But from a crease in his wallet, I'd emerged on the other side of his desk. We both stared curiously at the tiny photograph. God has a sense of humor—the unclaimed daughters and sons always come out with their father's near-sighted eyes or wide, luminous forehead. I had both.

"I didn't know about you until I was sixteen," I said. He looked puzzled.

"I was told you were dead," I clarified. It had never occurred to me that my father wouldn't know this basic fact.

A shadow eclipsed his fair olive skin. His glasses flashed in defense. "Oh," he said to himself. "Oh, that's not good."

"I kept this all along," he volunteered, his eyes glued to the photo as if it could make sense of what I'd just told him. "I even considered adopting sometimes," he continued, "but then I thought, no, I have a child."

I shuffled back to my room, registering the fact that my father, unbeknownst to everyone, had carried my image with him all along. I wonder if he shifted in his sleep, adjusting to the reality that for me he had been dead. Lying in the full-size bed in the guest room of my father's house, I slipped from the fluttering wings of pre-sleep to a deep slumber, thinking this first conversation was just the beginning, the preamble to a flood of emotions and explanations. Yet, inconceivably, those few awkward moments at my father's desk were the only ones we'd ever spend alone.

Today, Alejandro will call and I'll be out or the phone lines on the grid will blink red, signaling an electrical blackout in this part of the city.

He will fold, sort, and stack goods to take back to Cuba. His hands will pause between takeoff and landing and sketch a face on the foggy airplane window.

The server places a plate of lime wedges on my table. No evidence exists that I went to Cuba last night or that in six months I will risk everything to make a life with Alejandro. No evidence exists that a Cuban psychiatrist at the state hospital outside Maryland carried my photo with him for twenty years, that it was right there, pressed in his pocket along with his membership in the American Medical Association, his driver's license, and credit cards, that it was open and shut thousands of times over the years, never quite reaching the light. No evidence exists that this man was José Ignacio Alsina and that I'm his daughter. I'm the secret he carried in his billfold.

Later, in an e-mail, Alejandro will tell me he's been to France, Africa, and Mexico. Like a scholar, scientist, anthropologist, and diplomat with a government-approved Cuban passport, Alejandro travels quite easily. Even though Alejandro is a victim of geopolitics, even though he's economically disadvantaged and politically marginalized, he still fits into this tradition of travel. But some of us have traveled without invitations or guides. We've layered ourselves in scarves and shed them instinctively with only our hands for compasses. In this way, we can carve out a world in which we exist, a world where borders exist because we cross them, where journeys have value because we choose them. Little has been written about the female-shaped traveler, the young woman who will leave the United States, hoard Colombian pesos, and cross the Caribbean to convert those pesos into dollars and explore an embargoed territory.

Havana, 1999

On the way to Havana I'm braiding hair.

It's Semana Santa, Holy Week. I have a break from the university and I'm going to Cuba. The gate at Bogotá's El Dorado International Airport looks like a round, feathered corral of young swans in training. Dozens of girls from Bogotá's Ana Pavlova Academy are traveling to Havana for a classical ballet competition. They are all long limbs and self-possessed gazes, the older ones angling their necks as if the terminal were lined with mirrors. They stretch as they speak, dipping into gentle pliés as they nod. This band of girls traveling together projects an air of otherworldliness, but when we land in Venezuela for a layover and migrate around the same café and newspaper stand, I realize they are doing the same things all girls do—whispering furtively, then bursting into fits of giggles; swapping gum, hair ties, leg warmers, and nude lipsticks; and gawking at their surroundings.

The girls are chaperoned by three women, each one a decade or so older than the next. The women's knees are bowed with the arthritic stiffness of ex-dancers. They talk amongst themselves and occasionally call over one of the girls, whispering instructions into her attentive ear then sending her on her way. Besides a few stray businessmen, I'm one of the only people traveling alone, and a clique of four girls takes an interest in me. The girls, who look about ten or eleven, stare at me, talk amongst themselves, then stare some more. Finally, I smile and wave hello. An emissary in violet leggings ambles over and asks, "Did you braid your own hair?"

I nod and offer to show them how. The courageous one suddenly smiles shyly and looks down. I grab my bag and head over to where the others are sitting. I had been looking forward to reading and focusing completely on the trip, but in reality, I'm grateful for the distraction.

As I carefully brush and weave each girl's hair into a tight French braid, they tell me about their training, their school, and the competition. The four of them have straight, strong hair in different shades of chestnut. Plaiting one thick braid after another, I slowly recognize my own girlish crown beneath the dense hazel underbrush. I had dark hair with unlikely light streaks and whorls of cowlicks, knots, and tangles at the base of my neck. In Marshall, Missouri, a baby born with such thick, dark, tangled hair was an aberration. My mother never knew what to do with my hair, so she would drag me to the barber shop every several weeks to have my unruly mane lopped off. I swore the barber's eyes gleamed like the blade of his freshly sharpened shears when he got me in the chair.

I ask the girls about their families, and they bubble over with information. One father works in the Colpatria Building, one of the tallest in Colombia. One has a mother who sells emeralds and silver to fancy stores in Europe. Two of the girls say their parents are divorced. As I braid and look around, I notice a few girls whose stillness pools around them. Dancers cordon off parts of themselves—the turn of a wrist, a chin, or a jawline, parts that exist only for the stage—so that in real life they have a vague, almost vacant expression that might be mistaken for arrogance.

I too have left parts of myself to be figured out later, ignored parts I couldn't recognize in the mirror or be kind to. Now I've put all my hopes for reintegrating myself into this trip to a place called Havana. I suppose there will be buildings, roads, mirrors, and people. How much can I expect to discover if my father, my only link to Havana, is no longer there? Do I think someone will step from the shadows and lead me to a house with a photograph of an old woman whose hair is braided just like mine? What will the dead teach me? Am I crazy to think I can learn more from my father's city than I learned from him?

A voice over the loudspeaker prompts us to gather our things and form a line for immigration. The three women double-check each girl's documents, and everyone settles into silence. The long line of chestnut fawns fold their passports into brown leather pocketbooks and press them securely under their pointy elbows. Colombians are used to being frisked everywhere. Anyone can be pulled out of line, questioned, detained. Anything can happen when you show your papers.

While I don't run around with a fanny pack at my waist demanding ice in my water, I realize how characteristically American it is to assume I can go anywhere at any time. Until now, it's never occurred to me to think otherwise. One of the little girls looks over at me, a slightly worried expression beneath her crown of braids. I smile to reassure her but then realize she's concerned about me. Everyone, including me, is wondering if they will let the American travel to Cuba. But nothing happens. The official studies me, studies my passport, and puts a stoic Venezuelan stamp on it.

We board the plane and soon are on our way over the Caribbean to Havana. For the rest of the flight, I sleep deeply, as if I've sunk into the plane's cold belly. When I awaken, someone announces, "Welcome to Havana" and rattles off a string of weather and transportation details. I stifle the urge to laugh. The fact that Havana is presented the way any other tourist destination would be feels absurd and impossibly real at the same time.

At the José Martí International Airport outside Havana, I stand behind a thick, black line until I'm called forward. I step inside a booth encased in one-way mirrors. A window flips open and the bust of a thin, elegant black man dressed in olive drab appears. His high cheekbones arch like goblets beneath his Persian eyes. I answer the questions he addresses to me using my first name:

"What brings you to Cuba? How long do you plan on staying?"

"I'm here to see the lovely beaches. I will stay six days."

The customs officer looks up from my passport, examines my face, and looks down again. His amused, proprietary gaze fills the booth. "Where will you be staying?"

"I have a room at the Melia Cohiba."

"Have you made a reservation?"

"Oh, yes, I made my reservation weeks ago."

"I would like to see your return ticket, please." He enters something in a computer, then finally tells me, "Enjoy your stay." An automated lock clicks, and I step from the booth into an air-conditioned terminal, spotless, with gleaming luggage carousels and modern-looking scanning equipment. Unlike the ultra-serious Colombian security officials sporting semiautomatic rifles, Cuban guards slink around, apparently unarmed. They chat up the female airport workers, their skinny German shepherds excitedly tagging along. From the airport lobby, I call the number Alejandro sent me in a brief e-mail ten days before I left for Cuba. It turns out to be his work phone at the Center for Social Research. The woman who answers says he's gone for the day and won't return until Monday.

Did he forget I was arriving today? Could it be he doesn't know when Holy Week is? Indeed, we miss each other that first day. As I arrive at the airport, Alejandro leaves by train for his hometown, Caibarién, a fishing village on the north coast of the island. It's a Friday afternoon in March of 1999. Later, Alejandro will tell me how he lingered in his office for more than an hour before heading for the train station. He'll tell me he was afraid of what another meeting between us might bring.

I watch as an overly eager driver lunges for my bags and throws them in the back of the government-run taxi. The engine of the compact car turns over and hums efficiently. We are on our way into the city. From the window of the taxi, Cuba is much grassier than I had imagined. Red-and-black panels declaring *Socialismo o Muerte* and *Venceremos* loom blandly above large swells of weeds and snake grass waving along the side of the road. For as far as I can see, Cuba is a vast expanse of pale, anemic grass, some of it brown and scorched from lack of precipitation. Like a child, I'd imagined a Cuba that would pop up like a brightly colored, three-dimensional storybook. I remember the disappointment I felt the first time my mother, grandmother, and I crossed the Florida state line on a car trip from Missouri to Orlando. If anything, the landscape had gotten less lush, more barren, and browner as we rolled through Georgia into Florida. When our old Ford rattled across the state line and past a huge "Welcome to Florida, The Sunshine State" billboard with large navel oranges for *o*'s and a huge ocean wave curling over the word *Florida*, I felt deceived. There was no white sandy beach, no aquamarine water waiting for me.

Now, I just register my disappointment as a temporary visual experience because my sights are set not on Cuba, but on Havana. Havana is where my father's family has lived for many generations back, and Havana's what I've come for. I remember asking my father if his parents were from Havana and he said, "Yes, and their parents too, and so on. We're all from Havana." And when I asked him about other parts of Cuba, such as Oriente, his brow furrowed as if those other places were in a foreign country.

We continue passing stretches of pale yellow and brown grassy fields. Very soon, I will enter the capital for the first time. All the scorched earth in the world can't convince me otherwise. Havana, light inverted, shadow of my first thirty-two years. I'm meeting you in my adult life, just as I am learning Spanish. Strangely enough, in Havana's infancy, English was its dominant language. In 1762, Britain's King George III declared war on Spain, and a large British force captured and controlled Havana for a year until the British and Spanish governments made a trade: Florida for Havana. Soon, I will walk Havana's streets and possess every cognate that has migrated back and forth from English to Spanish—the "carnal" in *carnaval*, the "fort" in *fortaleza*, the "bell" ringing out in *bella*, the SOS in *sostener*. Soon, I will shear away the opaque sack of imagination concealing this city and its stones.

I look in the taxi's rearview mirror and see the airport fading on the horizon. For all of its modernity, its one-story, flat, rectangular shape resembles an abandoned army barracks. After several more miles of countryside, the road becomes more populated. A few miles later, we come upon more people: young women with plastic shopping bags and children hanging from their wrists; solitary bicyclists peddling furiously; a group of manual laborers staring blankly from the back of an old Chevy truck. People line up on dusty corners waiting for the *camello*, a long trailer that dips in the middle and is pulled by a diesel cab. Others saunter over and lean into the open car windows of antiquated Buicks and Chevys, trying to hitch a ride.

Niurka

A colleague at the Javeriana has connected me with his cousin, Teresa María, a young Colombian studying film in Havana. I go directly to Teresa María's house in Vedado, a suburb of Havana where she lives with a few other Colombians and her Swedish boyfriend, Jon. Teresa María takes me to Niurka's apartment a few blocks away. By the time we make it to the top of the stairs, Niurka is excitedly undoing the chain lock, deadbolt, and iron gate. Niurka, a thirty-something woman with wiry, haphazardly bleached hair, very fair skin and a large mole on her chin, greets Teresa María warmly with big hugs and kisses. She wears a snug-fitting, seventies-looking polyester pantsuit in lime green with large white circles.

Niurka holds out her hand to greet me, then gives me a kiss on the cheek and hurries us into the apartment. In a whisper louder than the average person's speaking voice, she warns that technically it's illegal to rent rooms to tourists: "The government charges so much in fees and permits, I can't afford to rent out a room the legal way, but since you're a friend of Teresa's . . ." she beams. At that moment, a thin, delicately boned young man steps into the hallway where we're standing.

"This is Javier," Niurka announces, then in a completely different tone, as if speaking a different language, she barks at him to make sure there's a pillow in the guest room. "Javi's studying to be a priest," she smiles at us.

We pass a room with two twin-sized beds. "This is where we sleep," Niurka explains. "And this is your room. I hope you'll be comfortable," she says to me as she steps into the room and smoothes out the floral-print bedspread. I say it looks great and place my suitcase in the corner.

"I'll make *cafecito!*" Niurka exclaims with a jolt. "You like café? I'm sure you must, being from Miami and all." She pulls Teresa María along by the wrist, chattering at breakneck speed like a child anxious to show an adult a new toy or discovery. Meanwhile, Javier explains to me that in Cuba everyone is very nosy, so I should try to be discreet.

"Well, won't they know I'm not from the building?" I venture.

"Oh yes," he affirms, "But just be discreet."

"I'm going to tell them you're my cousin from Miami," Niurka yells from the kitchen. Teresa María excuses herself and says she'll be back in two hours to take me out with her friends. Nothing seems discreet about my presence in this sunny, well-kept apartment as Javier, Niurka, and I sit to have our coffees, and they stare at me expectantly. "Is there enough sugar?" Niurka asks, leaning over and looking into my cup.

"Yes, it's delicious," I say, adding, "You make it just like we do in Miami." Then I pause, "Or I guess it's the other way around." We all laugh, and Niurka uses my blunder as an opening to proclaim that she has no hard feelings against the United States, something I'll find almost every Cuban does upon gaining the least bit of *confianza*, or trust. And it's just as Fidel has ordained, I realize later when I catch a few minutes of one of his sporadic speeches: "Make no mistake! It is not *el pueblo americano* [the American people] that we have a problem with. It's the U.S. government and the Miami mafia who want to destroy all that we've built!"

Despite Javier and Niurka's admonition that I should be "discreet," my presence seems something of an event, and I quickly realize one of the reasons why. As I'm unpacking my suitcase, Niurka knocks on my door and asks me to pay for the entire week's stay up-front. I tell her that's fine, and we negotiate an additional amount that I'll pay for food. She takes the folded bills gingerly and excuses herself. I can hear her in the adjoining room, burrowing around in the closet and opening boxes, no doubt hiding the money. Within a few seconds, she returns with a big floppy hat jauntily placed on her head and a canvas shopping bag looped around her forearm. "Let's go shopping!" she insists, "or I won't have sugar for your coffee in the morning."

I'm just back from the store with Niurka when I see Teresa María's enormous Buick pull up to the corner like a tugboat docking. I get in and greet Jon, her boyfriend, and the other two Colombians I met earlier, Camilo and Susana. We head off to one of Havana's oldest movie theaters, the Cine Chaplin, or El Chaplin, as people call it. The stark black mural of Charlie Chaplin tooling along with his cane against pristine, alabaster walls and the lobby's royal red carpet recall a time when movies were called "picture shows" and moviegoers were corralled into orderly lines by plush, red velvet ropes.

When we've taken our seats and the usher closes the doors, the theater goes completely dark for at least three minutes. I can't resist waving my hand in front of my face, but can't catch even a shadowy glimpse of it. Teresa María and her friends don't seem in the least alarmed, continuing to chat amongst themselves. Everything that's normally dark seems darker in Cuba. This cinema, devoid of aisle lighting, cellular phones, and radiating popcorn, feels like a cave. I stir in my seat and feel the air around me shift as if I'm underwater.

The film, *La vida es silbar* (Life Is to Whistle), centers on the story of three Cubans trying to fill fundamental voids in their lives: Mariana, a ballerina who never knew her parents, has an insatiable appetite for sex; Elpidio, a pot-smoking hustler, was abandoned by his mother (coincidentally named Cuba) and still waits for a sign of reconciliation from the Orishas, deities worshipped in the Afro-Cuban religion Santería. Julia, who as a young woman left her newborn on the doorstep of an orphanage, lives alone with a bevy of cats, parrots, dogs, and even a peacock. She faints every time she hears the word *sex*. Sex, spirituality, and solitude: as the movie unfolds, it appears that each character is unconsciously trying to recover family bonds through one of these.

The film presents Havana in Technicolor, except for brief archival clips in black and white of Bola de Nieve, Cuba's legendary Afro-Cuban jazz singer from the forties, who appears as the feckless Elpidio's alter ego. *La vida es silbar* is surprisingly critical of Cuban society. At one point, a psychologist who's treating Julia walks through Havana shouting words like "Sex!" and "Freedom!" at which pedestrians faint. A sense of confusion grows in me. Everything I've ever heard about Cuba has indoctrinated me to believe there's absolutely no freedom of expression there. It's clear the film is commenting on this repression, but how can it be that they're doing it from inside Cuba? When we exit, the sun has set and it's dark. Almost everything within a few blocks of the theater—buildings, streetlights, cars—is shut off, making me feel I'm still in the dark theater.

One of Teresa María's housemates, Camilo, offers to accompany me the few blocks from the cinema to Niurka's apartment. As we walk, he tells me about his experience studying film in Cuba. He jokes, "Cuba is for living movies, not for learning how to make them."

"How so?" I ask

"Well, the classes are all theory. We're in our third year and haven't even shot anything yet. There's no film, and even if we pay extra, it's hard to get." I remember a New York filmmaker once telling me he ran out of film in Cuba and had to beg a Canadian tourist to sell him video-cassettes so that he could finish his documentary.

We come upon a small building with a group of young people sitting outside. Muffled music vibrates on the other side of a door. A makeshift sign has been tossed on the ground facedown. No one is collecting money or officially guarding the door, so we go in. The building is constructed on a small incline, so we take four steps down as we enter, giving me the eerie feeling of entering a basement. The room, about eight feet by twelve, is packed. There's a bar, but nothing's being sold. The crowd feels unmistakably Cuban: Cuban rastas, Cubans in grunge, Cubans in Tommy T-shirts. A couple of guys are even wearing New York Yankees baseball caps. The sweet scent of hashish casually wafts through the space, along with the harsh, peppery smell of Populares, a cigarette brand I saw Niurka smoking earlier.

Behind a plastic window, two DJs work a single turntable. They stand on either side of it, their heads bent over, brows furrowed in concentration like two boys examining a hole in the ground. One DJ's dreads hang in a curtain around his face. He occasionally reaches over to a CD player, snatches out a CD, and drops in another without taking his eyes off the turntable.

The walls sweat and lean in toward the packed dance floor. Camilo and I pause at the edge. I place my hand on the wall's rough, unfinished surface and listen. The sound is not ubiquitous as it is in Miami's intricately wired clubs. It's highly centralized and shoots forth from the DJ booth in waves, like a cannon. I slip into the crowd and close my eyes, trying to get a feel for this music. Elements of hip-hop, rap, jazz, salsa, and techno are all recognizable, yet the combination is like nothing I've ever heard. Each musical element feels like a different hand scolding, blessing, caressing, and shoving the crowd. The primary bass beat is an enormous grizzly thumping. The secondary bass skips around lightly like a laser. The crackle of the turntable scratches and snags.

The people closest to the DJs start cheering them on, and the DJs break out a large, white plastic microphone, reminiscent of a Mister Microphone from the seventies. Amazingly, this caricature of a microphone manages to project the voice of dreadlock-DJ, who instead of the predictable shout-outs and roll calls, utters syllables and nonwords, repeating them over and over until they merge into intimate echoes and vowels. He plays with his voice, stretching out each syllable like taffy then giving it the low, nasal moan of a Tibetan chant. Without warning, the other DJ grabs the mike and breaks in energetically with words I can recognize, full-fledged sentences even, but he articulates them with an up talk, a polished, booming voice reminiscent of radio personalities of the fifties. He then switches to a military bark, and finally in his normal voice says something I can't make out.

I let my right hand flow from my shoulder. I move in counterpoint to the music, slowing down as it surges ahead. I lift my chin and elongate my neck and arms into clean, classical lines, but my waist and hips wave and wriggle like the tail of a fish weaving in and out of a reef. I invent. I improvise. I do exactly what I want, and no one pays the slightest attention to me. Camilo is close by, bouncing from one foot to the other. I move farther from him, wanting to lose all sense of Bogotá—its code of behavior and propensity for staring people into submission. It hits me that people aren't watching each other, not even those who appear to be dancing "together." A girl with rings on every finger cries out something that sounds part cheer, part insult as the DJs continue to move to a steady beat, their feet anchored firmly to the floor, their braids and dreads climbing, curling, and twisting toward the ceiling like dark ivy and tendrils, exposed banyan root and gnarled vine. Stacks of disks and albums cascade to the floor as their hands race around, grabbing LPs and adjusting the mike, which fades in and out.

I roll my shoulders and let my head fall to the side, circling, as I push my range of motion as far as possible. I move through elements of reggae, hip-hop, rap, and *son.* I am mesmerized, reinvented, and pushed completely to the edge of my own spontaneity. I've danced to fusion in Miami and Bogotá, but this feels completely different. The DJs' and the dancers' passion for improvisation is exhilarating and liberating. I lower my head and extend my arms to the side, my upper body swaying like a hammock between trees. My forehead meets with a mass of bouncy hair, and I look up to find a young guy with a commanding broad nose, delicate, translucent olive skin, and eyes of an indefinable light-colored shade. He doesn't acknowledge me but doesn't turn away either. We move closer and touch hands. The floor rises up to meet our shoulders, or perhaps we lower ourselves down. The wall sweats, and I imagine I'm inside a lung, the spongy walls and compressed air closing in, then expanding a little with each exhalation. I put my mouth on his, and it is warm, buoyant, and generous. A wave rolls through the crowd then recedes, pulling his shy smile toward the other side of the room. I make my way to the edge of the dancing crowd.

I wave goodbye to Camilo, signaling a reassuring "no, I'm fine" as he starts toward me to offer the obligatory walk home. Once I'm on the other side of the door, the vibrations recede to an uninteresting and mechanical sound, like a car engine being methodically tuned. I force myself not to look back. This place will be gone tomorrow. In its place will be a loose-skinned lady in curlers selling mayonnaise sandwiches, or a gaggle of bored mothers-to-be lining up for their allotment of iron-fortified powdered milk. For now, for just a few moments, I want to hold myself close to this place and to these Cubans whom I've been waiting to dance with for thirty-two years.

Hoping I'm going in the right direction, I grope for the key to Niurka's apartment and hold it in front of me like a flashlight. After a block or two, I recognize the corner of her building and the winding iron staircase. I climb one floor too high, backtrack down the stairs, and quietly let myself in, remembering Niurka's instructions to relock the iron gate as well as the chain and deadbolt.

When I'd asked her if the building was really that vulnerable to theft, she'd scoffed, "Oh no. No one around here robs strangers. In Cuba, you're more likely to have a friend go through your stuff while you're in the bathroom than to be robbed." I guess the locks are more to give a sense of privacy, which, in light of Niurka and her housemate's insistence that I "be discreet," seems to be completely lacking.

I slip into my room, and as soon as I sit down on the bed, my bones start to vibrate like an engine turning over. The rumbling of the plane, the flat questioning and deadpan persistence of the immigration officer, the heat, the walking, and the dancing in that dark room—all of it vibrates in my bones. I take a good look at my room. It's a simply furnished room, with a pockmarked wooden table and a long horizontal mirror that runs parallel to the bed. I undress and look at myself in the mirror. I open my mouth wide and imagine the light from a black-and-white movie flickering on the back of my throat. The light is jumpy and intermittent, as if emitted from an antique projector.

Why is black and white associated with truth, the severe lapel of history, the clean lines of documentaries, whereas color, which is closer to the actual appearance of the world, implies fantasy and fiction? Why did La vida es silbar's dark, grainy close-ups of Bola de Nieve's animated smile represent truth while the shots of contemporary Havana bordered on surrealism? It occurs to me that in the past several hours, I haven't thought of my father once. I'd expected to be suffused with a sense of him, or at least, of his absence, but now that I'm in Cuba, I feel nothing for him. I can't even conjure a thought of him.

I lie on the bed and feel my nakedness rise and expand toward the ceiling. I think I hear something, faraway humming or singing, but after a few minutes pass and the tone or volume doesn't vary, I realize I'm hearing silence. There are no cars, no airplanes flying overhead, no TVs blaring. I let this fact sink in: I am alone in this room, and nothing televised, broadcast, or human-made will reach me for the next several hours. Even more incredible is that this reality is not mine alone, but is shared by tens of thousands of people throughout the city.

In Havana, each sleeping body is its own background noise and each waking body its own traffic. In Havana, the moments pass according to each room's proportion and contents. Here, the minutes, seconds, and hours trudge through the long, horizontal mirror. They frolic in the floral bedspread's hydrangea and lilacs and waver before the four sallow walls.

My brain curls around this stillness as I sink into the sheets and blankets. I dissolve into the mattress, through the floor, into the foundation of the building. I bury myself in that first night. I sleep without memory of sleeping, oblivious to the ancient film still flickering against the cave of my throat.

Somewhere in Miami, my father is shifting and wrestling with his own dreams, trying to get comfortable between sanitized hospital sheets, hearing the beeping of an EKG and IV drip.

Alejandro

The next morning I wake up rejuvenated. I reach Alejandro at his office and we agree to meet later in the day, but first Niurka suggests that we go to a lecture by Micaela Chávez, an intellectual, scholar, and authority on Afro-Cuban religion who happens to be an old friend of Niurka's family. On our shopping excursion the day before, Niurka had shooed people from our path as if I were an invalid or a celebrity. Again today, I'm immediately lassoed into the submissive mode one assumes when going around with a domineering but harmless aunt.

In the quiet neighborhood of Vedado, we enter a *centro de cultura*, housed in a well-maintained, three-story colonial house, with marble floors and a winding staircase, that must have belonged to a wealthy family before the revolution. Just off the staircase, we enter a small, simple room that holds about fifty people, and someone hands each of us a lottery ticket. I realize with embarrassment that the lecture is already underway. Loudly whispering *disculpa*, Niurka makes a show of steering me to a seat, as the plastic shopping bag hanging at her side rustles with every step. She waves wildly at Micaela, who looks up from the paper she's reading with a wry expression.

The crowd, mostly women dressed in African prints and brightly colored headscarves, listens attentively, as I struggle to stay afloat in the undertow of academic discourse. I try to understand the gist of Micaela Chávez's words. Immersed in the polysyllabic flood, I frequently bob to the surface and catch the revolving terms *developed* and *undeveloped* world, *first* and *third* world. At the far end of each idea, the word *imperialist* sits, an omnipresent specter in Micaela Chávez's speech. It strikes me as antiquated and strange, a term that belongs in high-school history textbooks, but I'll learn that this word has become a mainstay of the Cuban lexicon over the last several years. Even nonacademic, everyday people use the term *imperialista* to refer to Cuba's meddling, self-serving neighbor to the north.

As Micaela finishes her talk, the crowd shouts out anxiously, "Don't forget the raffle!" The strange combination of intellectual elitism with childlike excitement surprises me. Micaela makes a few general announcements, then gets to the business of the raffle. She calls out a number, and a large woman sidles up to the front to collect her prize, a scarf that appears to be woven from the same ethnic patterns everyone's already wearing. Next, to my horror, my number is called. Niurka springs up from her seat joyfully, "Micaela! Micaela," she yells. "This is my friend from Miami!"

Micaela smiles politely. The crowd stirs and people in the first three rows crane their necks to get a look at me. Niurka chatters a mile a minute to the people sitting around us, "Imagine that! We just walked in and she won. Imagine!" She pushes me to the front of the room, where Micaela Chávez, predecessor to the legendary anthropologist Lydia Cabrera whose younger brother was Federico García Lorca's lover, ties around my neck a simple leather string with an amulet of Babalú-Ayé, the Afro-Cuban equivalent of San Lázaro. The crowd gives an obligatory round of applause while Niurka takes out my camera and starts shooting photos excitedly at breakneck speed, aiming the camera around the room randomly.

Afterward, we gather on the patio. Micaela Chávez is tall and distinguished, with ashen hair in a short, trim cut. She's also reserved, using different tones of voice with different people: distant to some and familiar, even jaunty, to a few. She says nothing to me, but I tell her it's an honor to meet her and apologize for entering the talk late. She looks at Niurka with the kind of measured patience that one who's not used to children might have for a child who is developmentally challenged. Soon a car arrives to sweep Micaela Chávez away. As the car drives off, she shouts to me, "I taught for a summer at Smith College! They know me there," and waves her hand in a shy, girlish gesture.

In front of the building where he works, *un centro de investigación* in a quiet Vedado neighborhood, Alejandro and I embrace like old friends. Alejandro's workplace is another elegant colonial home, much like the centro de cultura but a little more lived in. From the porch, I catch a glimpse of Spanish tile floors and a handsome, burnished wooden banister.

Alejandro still has the quiet, warm demeanor I remember. His eyes are the same indeterminate brown, but here in Cuba, his skin looks completely different. Under his short-sleeved, blue-and-gray plaid button-down shirt, his skin is a radiant, glistening bronze. Offering to carry my *mochila*, Alejandro situates himself between me and the street, and we start to roam the city. We walk all over Havana, talking, landing like birds in the street parks along the way. We stop at the University of Havana and sit on the steps outside the main building that houses the library.

"So what do you think of Havana so far? How do you feel?" he asks with a trace of uncertainty.

"It's amazing. I feel comfortable. Mesmerized by the light. It's a particular light."

He considers my statement: "Yes, I guess it is. I hadn't thought about it."

The stairs are regal and expansive, and the sun glaring against the white concrete makes everything painfully bright except for the small scar beneath Alejandro's right eye. That scar is my focus. In the background, I'm aware the stairs lead to marble columns supporting immense volumes of books. Here in Havana, the light alters my perceptions; typical scenes rearrange themselves in odd, new compositions.

Random details emerge as we wander around Havana. Alejandro remembers chasing land crabs as a kid in Caibarién, how they'd bury themselves head-first, then wiggle their tails, making waves in the sand. I tell him about the first time I ever heard a foreign language, French, in the line for a ride at Disney World. The experience of listening to a language only for its sounds, devoid of meaning, raised the hair on my arms.

We walk and talk for hours: Plaza de Catedral, Plaza de Armas, Plaza Vieja. We don't have a destination, and we don't discuss one. We alight in each plaza and sit perpendicular to the birds that line the walkways. A drunken man approaches. Looking from me to Alejandro, he takes off his Baltimore Orioles baseball cap. In a wide, sweeping gesture, he dismisses me and confides to Alejandro, I later learn: "Insist. Fight for her. She will say no, but you must insist." Then he shakes Alejandro's hand in a congratulatory manner, turns to leave, and mumbles, "Hang on to your criollita, hermano," as he staggers off. Between his thick accent and slurred speech, this last sentence is the only thing I understand. Alejandro blushes a little as he translates the old man's Spanish into his Spanish, pausing at the criollita part.

"I know what it means," I say lightly, to spare Alejandro the embarrassment of having to invent a euphemism, "but I do have a question about that word." I tell him I've looked up the definition countless times, and every dictionary says a *criollo* is a Spaniard born and raised in a Latin American country. He nods in agreement, but I know there must be more to this mysterious criollita word that has followed me here from Miami.

I've been accompanied almost every second since I arrived in Cuba, yet even so, men have shouted "Criollita" from across the street or mumbled it as I walk past. Yesterday in spite of Niurka's overprotective chaperonage, an elderly gentleman standing watch at the entrance of the *tienda de dólar* where we bought some food graciously said, "Tell your friend she's una criollita espectacular" and Niurka gushed, "Thank you, Señor."

"But what is a criollita?" I had pressed Niurka. The best she could come up with was, "It means you have a good body." The irony was almost comical.

"Do you realize that for as long as I can remember, I've been trying to disguise the fact that I have two bodies?" I tell Alejandro.

He looks surprised and slightly amused, "Where is your other body?" he says, pretending to search behind a tree. "And why would you want to hide it?"

From adolescence throughout my adult life, my hips and thighs have always been two, sometimes even three, sizes larger than my waist, shoulders, and chest. I've been mortified by this anomaly, in the same way I imagine a shy teenager with double-D breasts might feel. But in the small corner of America where I lived, large breasts were deemed a precious natural resource. The verdict was still out on big butts, but the long-legged women in Calvin Klein ads and lean, androgynous models of the eighties conveyed the message that a large, fleshy rear end and thick thighs ballooning from a tiny waist and upper body was closer to circus sideshow than physical asset.

Then, on my first trip to Miami, my father and Zoraida once followed me into a dressing room at Burdines, and she commented, "She has your mother's body," to which he assented. That gave me my first clue that my body shape might have come from my father's side—then came the term *criollita*.

"I understand that criollo means a racial mixture," I tell Alejandro, "but I don't understand what it has to do with a body type."

"The Criollita epitomizes what makes Cuba unique," Alejandro replies. "In our collective imagination, it's the perfect union between the Spaniard and the African."

"Aren't we talking about a big butt here?" I tease. "You're making this sound like a graduate thesis on postcolonial something-or-other."

"True, true," Alejandro laughs, blushing slightly. "I guess it does sound far-fetched, but it *is* a kind of postcolonial something-or-other. The image of La Criollita represents the merging of Cuba's primary racial groups: the idealized, ivory skin of a Spaniard wrapped around the romanticized, guitar-shaped body of a black woman."

In a few days, this duality described by Alejandro in such formal terms will be reiterated with graphic, unambiguous candor when I stop to buy a bottle of water at the bodega around the corner from Niurka's. As I turn to leave, the cashier whispers under his breath: "negra vestido de blanca" (black woman dressed in white). To my American ear, the term and the whole idea are loaded with latent racism and sexism, stirring conflicting emotions in me. Coming from a world where my body didn't reflect the ideal of white beauty and confused black people often asked me, "How can *you* be white?" it's a relief and a thrill to be with people for whom a dramatically disproportionate upper and lower body not only makes perfect sense but is considered beautiful.

Alejandro and I laugh and continue walking. I marvel at how relaxed and open I feel in this city. Despite the ever-increasing poverty, Cuba is still "safe." Alejandro explains that even the drunks are the friendly responsibility of the neighborhood. In Bogotá, it's unheard of to walk through the city with your purse hanging loosely at your side or to count money in public, but here, at least while I'm with Alejandro, no one feels menacing or remotely dangerous. Niurka told me the absence of crime in Cuba is due in part to unjustly harsh criminal sentences: fifteen years for petty theft, thirty years for solicitation. I feel uncomfortable that I might be enjoying liberties based on an unjust penal code, yet simultaneously I'm relieved that I can let my guard down and walk freely.

We continue walking, past a statue of José Martí, a bust of Lenin. We duck into a small store, and Alejandro buys a box of juice and a small package of cookies for us to share. He pays with dollars, handling each bill delicately, just as he did in Bogotá. We stop at El Paseo del Prado, a park located on the east side of Old Havana. Alejandro grabs my hand, and we take a seat on a bench beneath the shade of an enormous ficus tree where he says he used to read when he was in graduate school. In the late-afternoon sun, the tree-lined granite walkway of the Prado appears not to have aged in the least since then.

Groups of children scurry by wearing the national school uniform of red shorts, white button-down shirts, and red bandannas. Young men and women dressed in the brownish, mustard-colored uniforms of the state's high-school system laugh loudly and jostle each other playfully.

The boys' pants look like they've been let out as far as possible, yet the hems still graze their ankles. They shout and holler as the girls sashay by.

There are a lot of children and young people around, and they seem very independent. The children aren't ushered around by adults as they are in the United States. Two girls huddle over a folder, comparing notes. Several younger kids jump rope. Gaggles of schoolgirls pass by wearing long black skirts for flamenco class or pink leotards for ballet. Kids walk with loaves of bread tucked under their arms or stop on the corner, digging in their pockets to buy a soda or *guarapo* (juice extracted from sugarcane).

Havana strikes me as a city of children. Are these young people the *pioneros* I've heard about on international radio? Are they prototypes of the brainwashed, robotic kids that we were told Elián González would become if the U.S. government sent him back to his father? It was only the November before my trip that a woman had boarded a boat for Miami with her five-year-old son and twelve others. She drowned, but the boy survived and was handed over to relatives in Miami, who then refused to return him to his father in Cuba. Recent media coverage of the custody battle had put Cuba's pioneros in the spotlight. Cubans in Miami claimed it would be a crime against humanity to return the boy to a system that puts children in work camps and brainwashes them. I wonder if these kids have been taken to the countryside to harvest cane. Do they recite Martí's poem "Cultivo una rosa blanca" until it becomes a chant? Are they required to sign every composition with "Ten, twenty, thirty years *en la Revolución*"?

Even the adults possess a childlike quality. Men suck hungrily on stalks of sugarcane. Women's cackling laughter and tear-streaked tantrums breach all U.S. codes of conduct. The girls in their pionera uniforms have the wizened, vacant stares of old women, and the boys have the cracked heels and cold hands of old men. Many of their fathers are gone, Alejandro tells me, and their mothers are *resolviendo*, trying to make ends meet.

I tell Alejandro about my adventures in Havana so far, and he listens with great interest, raising his eyebrows and laughing at certain parts. As I'm telling him about going to the store with Niurka, my voice sounds carefree, jocular even, like an overconfident amateur stand-up comedian. I don't recognize my own voice. Alejandro doesn't seem to notice. I take a sip of juice to stop myself from babbling

"Whenever I start going on like this, it's because there's something else I really want to say. Something I'm afraid to say," I confess.

Alejandro looks surprised. Without intending to, I've made a dramatic shift. He looks down at the hand resting on his knee, takes a deep breath, and stares at me expectantly.

"Well, now I've set myself up to make some really important declaration," I laugh nervously, tempted to return to my glib monologue. "Look, I know we just spent one night dancing in Bogotá. . . ." My chest is tightening up as if someone's wrapped a rope around my ribcage. "Well, it's just that I feel a sense of familiarity with you." Alejandro's face softens and he nods in agreement. "I mean, here we are, and my heart is racing, and usually, I'd be completely second-guessing myself or wondering if you feel the same way, but with you. . . ."

Alejandro looks down at his hands.

"Well, I just know that you do."

He lifts a hand to his forehead and rubs his temples in a slow, soothing gesture, not like he has a headache, but in a gesture very personal to him and unfamiliar to me. He looks up.

"I'm married."

The ficus tree hovers. Each green, delicate oval darkens and tilts toward us. I want to run, to get up and tear through the rest of Havana in long, powerful strides. I want to be done with this place, to be done with Alejandro.

"Wow. I guess that's always a possibility," I say, looking down at my hands then forcing myself to look at him. I remember telling a coworker about my impending trip and the possibility of seeing the mysterious Cuban I met one night at the Goce Pagano.

"Be careful," she had said almost nonchalantly, "he may be married." I feel right now just as I did when she said it—like it was the most preposterous and obvious thing I'd ever heard.

Alejandro takes my hands and looks me in the eye, earnestly but with some detachment, like a doctor imparting a serious prognosis. "I've been married for many, many years and it's a complicated situation."

Alejandro's fingers are short, almost stubby. When I'd envisioned the man I might meet in Havana, he had long fingers and strong, wide hands, sunbaked palms and pensive knuckles. But here I am with this unimagined hand in mine. I touch his scar. Is that a place where his marriage got "complicated," or is it the only small nick on his body still untouched by marriage? There is nowhere else to be but in this moment, my hand beneath the scar below Alejandro's right eye, the shade of the ficus descending. It's getting dark. We talk, moving closer and closer as if people are listening. One hundred thirty pesos to the dollar, land crabs making lines in the sand, a project he and his work group want to do without government funding. We move closer and keep talking until our mouths wrap around the same word. Our lips meet in the articulation of the same syllable and grow silent around the center of the word, where the vowel waits like a well, pulling us inward and downward. We embrace, our foreheads bent low in the last light.

I don't know yet that one of Alejandro's teeth is throbbing. I cannot see the abscess in his mouth or the left testicle rubbed raw from the last few years of riding into Havana six miles each way every day on a seventy-five-pound Chinese bicycle. It is twilight—the moment between afternoon and nighttime. Borges, whose eyesight waned for many years before he went completely blind, writes about blindness as an "eternal twilight," where the blues veer into sharp hues before becoming hazy. Borges doesn't describe blindness as the absence of colors or shapes, but rather as the presence of this dusky, twilight blue. Borges' images, shapes, and colors did not disappear; they were overshadowed.

We shuffle in silence toward Niurka's. My feet ache from all the walking. Sweat trickles down my neck and between my shoulder blades. My energy has drained into a state of relaxation bordering on exhaustion, the way I felt the night we danced in Bogotá. This moment with Alejandro slowly grows beyond awkwardness. It fills the little rented room despite the fact that he's married and, as an American citizen, I shouldn't even be here. Like Borges' tentative sight tinged with the blue of racehorses, cornflowers, and marbled ceilings, a deep pleasure emerges from the hazy twilight.

Later, I will learn about the failed marriage, the projects that are never realized because they are not sanctioned by the government, and the physical discomforts of poverty—constant stomachaches, bad teeth, ingrown toenails, and calloused feet—but for now, we've arrived at the foot of the well-made bed in my rented room. We are two people bent over the foot of the bed, taking off our shoes, two people at the point of making love, two people empty of desire. On the verge of making love, I'm empty of desire and bewildered by my own emptiness.

"I don't know if I can do this," Alejandro says. He tells me that he has had a few "flings" and even fell in love once. He says if he moves forward, he might never be able to return. He refers not to his marriage, but rather to the ambiguity surrounding it, which has sustained it for the last five or six years. Twilight brushes up against the side of the building on Linea and Fifty-Third. It hovers over the boatlike Chevys and Buicks that occasionally rumble by in slow motion below our window. Losing the shapes, colors, and images, we embrace, the weight of our arms circling each other, our foreheads nudging the early-evening shadows.

He reaches for me. I reach back to him from Louisville, Kentucky, where my grandmother once held up an afghan she had crocheted and made the pronouncement: "You'll only love one person like this." The pattern of triangles connected in a geometrically perfect design symbolizes that the lover and beloved are two halves of the same body, that there's only one "right" person for each human.

The pattern revealed between my grandmother's crooked thumbs startled me. I knew I was expected to praise her handiwork, but something perturbed me about its exact proportions and unyielding symmetry. I told her the afghan she'd crocheted was pretty. I wanted to tell her that I suspected love was neither perfectly symmetrical nor geometrically exact. Now I realize she wasn't prophesying but excluding me from her worldview.

Later I discovered that my grandmother considered my birth a double transgression. My mother told me this one Christmas on the drive home from Kentucky. She was widowed at age twenty-four when her husband died of kidney disease; her parents came, gathered up her things, and took her home to live with them, her mother proclaiming, "You'll never love anyone else like you did your husband." So a second relationship and a baby born from that relationship was a disgrace carved on the cold gray tablets of my grandmother's cosmology.

Alejandro reaches for me. The more he reaches, the less I recognize the shore where I once knew pleasure and could swim to it purposefully under almost any circumstance. My body was once arranged, alphabetized, punctuated, and defined by pleasure. A kiss I swallowed. A dance where I lowered myself through the skin of a drum to its floor, then pulled myself up by the strings of the guitar's melody. A bite that turned me into an apple. A knife that turned me to meat. Now my body is empty of desire. I'm inert and awkward.

Instead of the erotic, tender places, I want to touch all of the parts of him most worn down by the earth—his elbows and heels, the outsides of his hands. I want to comfort him. We sit on the well-made bed. We bend over our unlaced shoes. We talk through the night. Our words enter each other's mouths and vanish. There are so few cars in Cuba that the night is perfectly silent. I open my mouth, not sure whether to say "I can't do this" or "I must do this," but they mean the same thing. In the little room with the simple table and horizontal mirror, we both agree to return to our previous lives. I draw in a breath to beg, refuse, and wonder, but embrace Alejandro instead. Best to stay in the present. Best to keep my body at the center, a fulcrum between the past and future.

The sea is for goodbyes and the Malecón, Cuba's battered seawall, is the platform where all the city's goodbyes take place—the obscene, the tender, the absurd, and the inevitable. Gabriel García Márquez has come here, so have prostitutes and their European clients, mothers with their sons. A billboard just off the Malecón near the U.S. Interests Section (the de facto U.S. embassy in Cuba) boasts a representation of a robust Fidel clad in olive drab staring defiantly across the Florida Straits at a rickety Uncle Sam figure. The billboard reads, "Imperialists, we aren't in the least bit afraid of you." Alejandro says that his coworkers always interject, "What we are is envious." We laugh and look around. A few cars pass by. Here and there couples dot the wall, intermittently embracing and talking. Men stand alone, casting out lines without bait. From several yards away, two men and a woman approach. The men carry inner tubes. They throw them over and jump the wall. Their thin, tanned arms and legs are splayed outward and tensed as they cautiously inch across the sharp rocks like crabs. Each man mounts his inner tube, as the woman standing at the edge of the wall looks down on them, concerned. She waves a white handkerchief and smiles, feigning cheerfulness. "Are they . . . ?" I ask Alejandro.

He shrugs and smiles sheepishly. The woman continues to wave, but the men aren't going anywhere in particular. They simply float in their inner tubes, chat with each other, and occasionally look up at her. We walk on and stop at a less-populated section of the wall. I can't believe I'm only ninety miles from the tip of Florida. The sea looks so vast; the number 90 is compact in comparison: the nine looks like a body curled on its side; the zero, a rounded cove of water. Alejandro wraps his arm around my waist. His skin radiates warmth. We watch the choppy aquamarine waves stammer toward the silent, placid surface beyond. I'm glad I'm not going back to Miami immediately. In Bogotá, I can wrap myself in gray wool and dark, woven cottons. I can ignore the ocean for a while. Miami doesn't let you mourn but rather insists that you shed your clothes and soak up its oils, humidity, and exhaust.

The day I most needed to mourn, Miami's sun was unforgiving. The sun and my father's gleaming white Buick glared relentlessly, so that I got out of the car without really seeing it, but I heard my father's wife open the trunk and slam it resolutely. I felt her thrust the canvas strap of my carry-on into my hand. It was July 1990, a few years after my original visit.

I had landed a two-week volunteer gig with Catholic Charities, working with Haitian refugees. I saw it as an opportunity to regain contact with my father after calling and writing periodically with no response. I thought if I showed up in Miami, they would have to receive me. I also thought, being older than at the last visit, I could handle the situation more maturely, but lunch with them at La Casita on Eighth Street had validated my sense of dread: his wife, Zoraida, would never let me get close to him. When I said I would love to move to Miami, she said they were moving to Puerto Rico. When I said there might be a job for me at the Haitian American Organization, she pinched her face in disgust and asked why in the world I'd want to work with *los negros*. On the way back to my hotel, we stopped at their house for coffee. They had redone the patio, covering the small backyard patch of grass with gleaming mausoleum-white tiles. Even still, ivy crawled up the fence; the neighbor's palm leaned over the gate like a giraffe lazily chewing grass. Beneath our feet, the tiles shone, reflecting the sun as the ocean does at midday. I could hardly see, much less pose, so I didn't. Neither did he, and the photo reflects it—both of us tired: tired of being connected, tired of being strangers.

A young woman on a bicycle approaches Alejandro and me. The gleaming sun glares off her forehead and shoulders. Her dark skin glows a deep midnight blue, and her long, shining braids swing with her movements as she pedals by with her knees turned provocatively outward. She's bicycled past us two or three times now. I start to ask Alejandro about her, but he smiles indecipherably and looks toward the sea again. Do I see shame inverted and refocused in this slight smile? Is he embarrassed to see parts of his city through my eyes: the fifteen-year-old prostitute; the drunken homeless man; the fact that if we stop wandering and decide to sit somewhere to eat, the radical disparity in our economic situations will leap to the foreground and could overshadow our connection?

What I interpret as shame or embarrassment turns out to be desire. Alejandro's desire can be traced back to the twelfth-century Middle French root of *desire*, derived from "to miss." Before its meaning of longing, and way before lust, *desire* meant to be lacking something. "Añoro mi matrimonio," Alejandro tells me, taking both my hands into his and facing me. "I miss my marriage," he emphasizes, squeezing my fingers tightly as he enunciates the *ñ* in *añoro*, which makes the same *y* sound as the double *ll* in *llorar*; it's true, *añoranzas*, this rumbling, molten amalgam of missing, longing, and lacking, can erupt from deep in the throat and burst to the surface in tears.

Alejandro tells me about his wife's hand unjeweled and glittering, her fingers splayed above the dried black beans spread across the surface of a wooden table. She used to pick through the beans, flicking away tiny stones and twigs like an ancient mathematician on an abacus, clicking her way through the phases of the moon or charting planets based on the location of the stars.

"My wife used to question things," he confides. Long before the backs of park benches were removed to discourage Cubans from "congregating," his wife's shoulders started to slouch, and she became disinterested in debate and discussion. "On our third date, she said to me, 'I don't know if I'll ever love you, but I will marry you.'" Alejandro says this almost wistfully, then explains, "Her questioning made it seem there was more possibility for love than if she had just declared her feelings outright."

I wonder if I'm supposed to play the role of the wise consort and say something insightful, but he continues, answering my unspoken question. "I'm thinking of this now because I realize I miss something I've never had and never will have." Once he traces his feelings to their origin, he's angry at himself and at the wife who has told him numerous times she will not relinquish their marriage. For a long time, I attributed my not having a relationship with my father to the fierce hold his wife had over him, but an instinct I didn't want to acknowledge always said our relationship, and the lack thereof, was ultimately his decision, not hers.

We move farther along the wall toward the street that will take us to Niurka's. Alejandro wraps up his story by saying that after a few years of marriage, her inquisitive nature rebelled against teaching rote revolutionary dates and calculations to high-school students. So in the eighties, when things in Cuba were better economically, she declared she wanted to be a housewife. That's when he first felt he'd really lost her.

Alejandro seems to relish these connections and realizations. He doesn't struggle against them as I have seen a lot of men do when talking about interpersonal relationships. And I am strangely comfortable in the role of confidante. I imagine myself having the exact same conversation in the roles of wife, daughter, sister, lover, and friend. With Alejandro, every role leads to the same feeling of calm and familiarity.

The salsa music blaring from a snack bar across the street echoes hollow and tinny against the rush of the waves. I look behind me and can barely make out the distant form of the midnight girl, now walking without her bike.

Alejandro and I return to the narrow room and its horizontal mirror. We arrive at the twelfth-century meaning of desire and stretch out quietly with our deficiencies and hunger splayed about the floral-print bedspread. I sit up and catch a glimpse of myself in the mirror. I look like a child with my bare arms and simple summer tank top. With my rumbling belly; wide, curious forehead; and braids frizzed from sun, sweat, and the dust that rises from the cracks of the broken sidewalks, I look more like a girl-child than a woman.

We work our way to the present moment: the edge of the twentieth century, where I'm stronger than I ever thought I could be, where we meet unafraid. I'm capable of touching myself and being touched. I'm capable of any sound and any color of blue. We wrap around each other without blankets or sheets, without pillows or light or dark. This is the galloping I remember from the *son*. We stay close to it, but give it room to lead us, and this final time, we shudder with the swagger, the hunger, and the comforting solitude. For the moment Alejandro is not hauling buckets of water up and down stairs for a child's shallow bath, and I'm not wandering the streets my country has outlawed. Our feet don't ache. Our throats aren't parched. Below a window that's even quieter than we are, we discover the moment's delicate secret: inside each other, we are outside ourselves.

Bogotá

I'm waiting for Alejandro at Bogotá International Airport. It's July—midwinter in Colombia—damp and frigid. People pour from the arriving flights into a drab concrete holding area just outside the terminal. Men in business suits pace and bark into their cell phones. Guards armed with semiautomatic rifles stand off to each side of the crowd, staring ahead impassively. Taxi drivers queue up, waiting impatiently for fares. Entire families of six and seven children wait, scrubbed spotless and buttoned into the lace dresses and miniature suit coats of first communion, to pick up a father, uncle, or grandmother.

It's after 10:00 p.m. I've never picked up anyone at the airport so late before. What if he doesn't show up? What if I don't see him amidst the shadows of gray coats pushing, shoving, and jostling? We agreed on this visit matter-of-factly. A few weeks after my Semana Santa trip, we spoke on the phone. I asked him when he could come, and he said he could get away from work for the month of July. We agreed on the trip in neutral tones. Now almost three months have passed, and I'm petrified, wondering what I've gotten myself into.

Alejandro touches my shoulder, and I jump. His head is shaved. He's wearing a thin, long-sleeved shirt and clutching a small canvas tote bag, the kind one would pack for a weekend or overnight trip. With his head shaved, his eyes and forehead look larger, exaggerated almost. He smiles and explains, "It's sweltering in Cuba right now." I'd expected to be nervous, but my generalized anxiety quickly intensifies into an acute sense of regret. What is he doing here? What was I thinking when I asked him to come? A pack of cab drivers weaves in and out of the crowd, shouting destinations and prices. I absentmindedly confirm the fare with the first one I see, and we get in. The shock of Alejandro's unfamiliar presence temporarily distracts me from my own self-consciousness. I currently have the worst case of acne I've ever had in my life. A few days ago, I started to get one blemish then another, and within twelve hours my face was covered in acne, my skin bumpy and pink. Finally, one of my students' parents, a dermatologist, agreed to see me between patients. He shone a lamp on my face, took a quick look and quickly scribbled out a prescription for an ointment and some pills. I thought I had some kind of rash or skin condition, but he declared it a standard case of stress-induced acne.

Alejandro doesn't seem to notice when he touches my cheek tentatively and says, "You look beautiful."

It was easy enough to get him here. Cuba doesn't mind letting intellectuals go to places like Colombia. The countries are friendly. As one of my colleagues joked, "Cuba is like Colombia's mistress. She's the one he really loves, but when the United States (the official wife) comes around, she gets pushed into the back room." I paid for the ticket, and one of Alejandro's Colombian friends who works for a nonprofit human rights organization wrote him a letter of invitation to a fictitious conference on human rights in Bogotá. In the cab, I make small talk with the driver, something I never normally do.

I'm grateful my roommate is out of town, because reacquainting myself with Alejandro would be even more stressful with others present, but as I unlock the door and enter the cold, silent living room, I wish there was already some activity going on that we could just fall into. The room is dormant but charged with energy, like a darkened stage: what's to take place has yet to unfold. A futon mattress slumps delinquently against the far wall, a low walnut table crouches in the corner, and my roommate's cherished collection of Andean flutes hangs bound together on the wall like an ancient mask. I leave the lights in the main room off and turn on a lamp in the kitchen. When I return, Alejandro is standing in front of the empty fireplace. I've never built a fire—my roommate always does it—but all the accessories are there. Alejandro reaches inside and finds the gas switch. We stack some logs and crumple up little pieces of newspaper. It feels good to be doing something simple and necessary together. At first it's a paper fire of wild blue tongues and little sparks that quickly disintegrate to ash, but finally one of the larger logs catches and smolders to a slow-burning, deep orange flame.

"Can we just be quiet for a while?" I ask Alejandro as we settle on the thin carpet in front of the fire.

"Of course," he smiles broadly and squeezes my shoulder, but when he turns back to the fire, I catch a glimpse of his unguarded face out of the corner of my eye. The flames are not large enough to throw shadows, but they do cast a warm amber light across Alejandro's face, which is tilted slightly downward in reflection or sadness. I'm not sure which.

Carulla

Carulla, Bogotá's largest chain of grocery stores, boasts the well-stocked shelves, wide aisles, and glistening produce sections one could find in any U.S. supermarket. As we enter, I ask Alejandro to grab a cart while I hurry to the produce section to look for grenadines. After a few minutes, I glance over and see him standing in front of the shopping carts, sizing them up as if they came in different models. Finally, he chooses one, places his hands on the sides of the cart, and wiggles it out of its space. Once he gets the hang of how to wheel it around, he steers far out of the way of the other shoppers, making wide, clumsy turns beyond the periphery of the aisles. "We don't have carts allá," he comments. "Only baskets." Alejandro almost never refers to the island by its proper name. Unless he is asked directly where he's from, he calls it "allá." Cuba is always "over there," unnamed, yet ever-present. He says that even people with dollars wouldn't buy enough at one time to need such a large cart. I explain that a lot of people buy their food for the entire week in one shopping trip.

"Hmm," he says, looking unconvinced.

We continue shopping. I ask Alejandro to grab a head of lettuce while I look for sweet potatoes. I glance over a few times as I make my way from potatoes to onions, celery, and apples. Alejandro stands in deep concentration before a lush, leafy green splay of romaine, red leaf, butter leaf, and chard. A few minutes later, he appears smiling, his right hand wrapped triumphantly around an unpackaged head of iceberg lettuce. He's gripping it so tightly the muscles in his left shoulder and neck are visibly tense. The translucent green globe dangles by his side. Some layers curl into dark green; others are almost white, their thin leaves beaded with microscopic drops of precipitation. It comes from the outskirts of Bogotá, where farmers barely manage to salvage a third of their crops. The guerrillas often bury broken-up chunks of coal in the fields to render the land infertile and push the peasants off their land. But at this moment, the triumph is Alejandro's. Later, I will wonder how choosing a head of lettuce could be such a big deal for a philosopher, but in this moment, I see him in the entirety of his journey: he's come from heat, glare, and hunger, temporarily leaving everything familiar behind for the momentary pleasure of making a choice.

I slip my arms between Alejandro's cotton shirt and the insulated lining of the jacket I've lent him. I embrace him. Not a hug (arms wrapping around bodies), but an embrace, a moment encircled and briefly suspended. When we arrive at the checkout counter, Alejandro pushes the cart past the conveyer belt, the cash register, and the surprised bag boy. With no thought of paying or even emptying the cart, he just keeps walking. I thought it would be a novelty for him to see a real supermarket, but I could never have imagined how central Carulla would become to Alejandro's one month in Bogotá and our time together.

Bread. Wheat. White. Egg. French. Raisin. Challah. Italian. Bran. Rye. Sesame seed. Poppy seed. Dried onion. Bread sprinkled with sugar. Bread with sea salt. Garlic. Pumpernickel. Almond. The first time I put bread on the table, Alejandro picks off some of the dried onions curiously, but pushes the basket away. He then places the basket on the opposite side of the table—so far it teeters on the edge—and picks up his knife and fork. Later, when he goes to the kitchen for salt, he takes the bread with him, carefully wrapping it in plastic for safekeeping. Upon seeing my curious expression, he explains, "Bread is what we eat when there's no food."

Yogurt. Strawberry. Banana. Pineapple. Guava. *Maracuyá. Lulo.* Peach. Apricot. Cherry. Yogurt with nuts. Yogurt with fruit on the bottom. Yogurt with fruit blended in. Yogurt with cereal. Firm yogurt. Smooth yogurt. Drinkable yogurt. High-fat, low-fat, nonfat yogurt. Alejandro says that "allá" they are allotted one liter of yogurt a month. "It's nondairy," he adds. "Not like this yogurt." When I ask him what flavor he wants, he confides that he can't quite wrap his mind around the concept of flavors and varieties. "What is the difference exactly?" he asks.

"Well, there are different flavors, brands, prices, and sizes." I explain again, this time adding that sometimes several different flavors are even all packaged together. "Variety packs, they're called."

It's not just the abundance that baffles him, but how it is organized and presented to the consumer. After all the reading and writing he's done about consumer culture, he's not prepared to be a consumer himself, and although he's traveled frequently, he's not used to buying and preparing food. On his previous trips to other countries, people have simply fed him and driven him around. "I haven't really been involved with the praxis of the food," he jokes. Praxis, or the practical application of theory and knowledge, is a word he uses frequently.

Alejandro explains that food has always been so central to the Cuban idea of family and community that without it, the concept of sharing has become symbolic. His work group regularly collaborates with other groups. There are endless neighborhood meetings, gatherings, and events, but always with little or no food, and as Alejandro points out, a Cuban event without food is unimaginable "Even now," he adds, referring to the Special Period. "It's like we're playacting at teamwork," he confides, because deep down everyone's worried about how they're going to eat. Eating happens on the sly—a piece of boiled yucca and some beans prepared hastily for the children, a quick sandwich of bread and mayonnaise devoured before the long bicycle ride home. The more I hear about Alejandro's daily life in Cuba, the more I take pleasure in his newfound appetite. I gather ingredients to reintroduce old flavors to his palate as if I am reuniting long-lost family members.

We buy raisins to make *picadillo*, a Cuban dish made with ground beef. I know true picadillo has not existed in Cuba for decades, as beef has been completely unobtainable. Cows are strictly regulated by the government. Alejandro tells me that in the countryside when a cow dies, a medical examiner is called as if it were a criminal death. If the cow is found to have been murdered (some people "accidentally" run over cows for their meat) the perpetrator can be sent to prison. He remembers that his mother used to make picadillo with raisins, Spanish olives, capers, and a twist of lime.

I deposit him in the meat section and go to look for raisins. When I return, I find him studying the various packages of meat, comparing prices. I look for olives. I look for eggs. I do the rest of the shopping with the meat section as my nucleus. When I've finished, I find a package of ground beef that looks like the quantity we need, toss it in the cart, and tug on his jacket as a signal that we're done.

I quickly learn it's faster and less frustrating to leave Alejandro in the section of the store he finds most intriguing while I do the shopping. It's usually the meat section, but one day he spends an hour looking at all the varieties of toilet paper—two-ply, quilted, scented, recycled, jumbo, and hypoallergenic. He calculates the number of squares per roll and the price of each square of toilet paper, multiplying the amount times two if the paper is two-ply. He concludes that the two-ply toilet paper on sale is not the best deal.

"In the end, you get more for your money with the item that appears to cost more," he explains excitedly, having found a flaw in the logic of the sale.

"Well, sales aren't created to save money anyway. They're created to sell more stuff," I reply, realizing how maniacal this sounds in my bare-bones translation.

"What do you mean?"

"Well, I mean it's a marketing ploy," I don't know the word for marketing in Spanish, so I say *márketing* with an accent in the hope he might recognize it. Later, I will discover that *márketing* is indeed a word in Spanish, but Alejandro is not familiar with it.

"Marketing?" Ashamed of my own impatience, I tell him it's too complicated to explain. We move on.

In Cuba during the eighties, there was enough food to fill the refrigerator, enough to have eggs, ham, and cheese several times a week—and milk for the children. In 1989, the Germans tore down the Berlin Wall, the Soviet Union began to collapse, and millions of dollars in subsidies that had kept Cuba afloat for three decades rapidly evaporated. Food flew off the shelves and simply never reappeared. Alejandro explains this in a modest, concerned tone as if it had happened to someone else.

This is the same detached tone I heard on the phone when he warned me of his stomach problems. "I can't eat really," he had said, his neutral voice wilting into shyness. He went on to describe a stomach condition that prohibits him from eating anything but small quantities, and when he does eat, he often has severe stomach pains and indigestion. I suspect that since 1991, his "condition" has been poverty, but one day when we are lugging our grocery bags from Carulla to the apartment, he clarifies that it started way before the Special Period.

"My mother used to call me 'special,'" Alejandro laughs, "which is code for a pain in the neck when you have seven kids and one of them won't eat what you put on the table." We're going to try to make paella, and Alejandro's mesh bag is filled with plastic bags of squid, shrimp, and calamari that swish with each step. Alejandro says he remembers having stomach problems as far back as the age of nine.

"On Friday and Saturday nights, my mother would drag me through town, looking for my father," he says. His brothers were already in their preteen or teenage years, and his baby sisters were too heavy to carry.

Alejandro was the perfect size for these expeditions—old enough to walk on his own, yet young enough to inspire sympathy from spectators.

"We'd enter every taverna in Caibarién, and when my mother found him . . ." he flicks his wrist with a snapping sound and raises his eyebrows for emphasis. He paints a picture of his mother crashing into tables and pushing women off her husband's lap. She'd throw his glass to the ground, grab him by his collar, then face the bar's patrons, legs and shoulders squared off, and denounce him.

"My mother had barely an eighth-grade education, but she could come up with some poetic verse," Alejandro remembers. "She'd shout something like, 'Horacio, the unfit father, the drunk, the cheat—Horacio whose cotton shirts are woven with the sweat and fallen hairs of whores.'"

All of this without ever letting go of little Alejandro's wrist.

"What did you do? How did you feel?" I ask, squeezing his arm.

"That's when my stomach started to hurt."

These regular appearances became so much a part of the bar's repertoire that the bartender chose to treat Alejandro and his mother like patrons, knowing that to try to throw them out would cause even more of a ruckus. He would offer little Alejandro a ham sandwich, which Alejandro would always decline by solemnly lowering his head. No one would have guessed from the boy's mild-mannered demeanor that inside, his intestines were lurching and coiling, contracting and rolling themselves into a ball like a pair of boa constrictors.

We arrive at my apartment, and I hand Alejandro my bag while I fish for my keys. "Back then, this was common," he says, referring to his father's philandering. "But I always knew it was wrong, and the revolution, while full of contradictions, did proclaim woman's equality with men and, in theory at least, denounced that kind of behavior."

I wonder if the revolution would denounce Alejandro for being here with me, but I have a more urgent prerevolutionary question. My mother always described my father as someone who seemed to feel entitled to as many women as he wanted. They went dancing frequently, and whenever I'd ask if he was a good dancer, she'd say, "Your father preferred to be alone in the middle of the dance floor with everyone looking at him than to be dancing with me."

"Why do you think your father chased so many women?" I ask.

Alejandro pauses to consider the question, "Because he could."

One Sunday, I start to make picadillo, and I ask Alejandro where he put the raisins. He smiles bashfully and stands in front of the refrigerator as if to block the way. He opens the refrigerator door cautiously and starts moving packages to the side and lifting jars carefully. Opening the produce drawer, he pulls the small plastic package of raisins out from behind a package of limes and underneath a small pyramid of green apples.

He takes one out gingerly and places it in my mouth. "We won't need many for the picadillo," he explains, placing a raisin in his own mouth as well.

"And if we do, we can buy more," I state flatly. Sometimes I'm moved watching Alejandro explore this world of flavors, variety, and comparison shopping. Other times it's exasperating. Where food's involved, our interactions have a mute, underwater feeling. I'm pulled into an oceanic existence where packages of pork sausages and dried apricots float by so slowly we must acknowledge them as if they were new discoveries. I realize this is a rite of passage for Alejandro, this transition from a world of sugar water, beans, and gray soy meat to one of six kinds of apples, twelve cuts of steak, and twenty-three varieties of cheese. What I don't understand yet is that it will be a rite of passage for me too.

Within a couple of weeks, Alejandro's pallid, drawn face looks robust and all references to his stomach condition have vanished, but I have become increasingly disturbed. Like the travel ban of the late nineties, the U.S. embargo against Cuba is rarely discussed in Miami. Although I've always been of the opinion that it's ineffective and unfair, I've never had strong feelings about it. Witnessing Alejandro's first experience of abundance prompts conversations about the grinding poverty Cubans have experienced, especially since the Special Period.

I start to read about the embargo, and my worst fears are confirmed: not only does the United States enforce a strict trade embargo with Cuba, it punishes other trading partners for selling products to Cuba. I gradually develop a deep resentment against the embargo and its effects on the Cuban people.

It's hard not to recognize the David and Goliath metaphor in this tiny island literally being starved by the world superpower only ninety miles away, and one thing I'll quickly learn is that it's one of Fidel Castro's most frequently used rhetorical devices to garner support against *el imperio*. But in Cuba, I discover people are far more savvy than that. Everyone refers to *el bloqueo* almost the way one would talk about severe thunderstorms, but if you listen closely, they also criticize Fidel Castro's use of it. These people truly are caught in the middle and have a much more nuanced understanding of the issues than your average American or Cuban American—perhaps because they're living the reality.

Sometimes I return to our shopping cart to find Alejandro trying to strike up conversations with fellow shoppers or store employees. I hear him lamenting the price of fresh salmon or comparing the prices of ground beef versus ground pork. He's trying on the voice of a shopper. The other shoppers smile politely and move on. The supermarket employees lean in and listen to him attentively until they realize that he doesn't actually have a question about a particular product. His questions are rhetorical—postulations about the carnivore and the consumer. His cravings are existential, but they are also physical.

Whatever frustration I feel under the glaring lights and in the slow lines of Carulla dissipates when we are at home, where Alejandro and I cook, eat, and talk about food with a pleasure that is simple and self-contained. This plate of rice and seasoned meat. This custard sprinkled with ground cinnamon. This apple sliced into one's hand.

In the mornings, we take the bus together to the Javeriana, where I'm teaching a summer course. He looks around the shops or reads while I teach class, then we go home to prepare lunch together. For this month in Bogotá, our meals are meeting times, spaces we enter in order to exchange, to embrace, to give, and to receive. We eat breakfast by candlelight. We even celebrate boiled things—boiled eggs and yucca, boiled coffee and milk. Sometimes we start talking about the next meal before we've finished eating the current one. At night in the dark, we drift off to sleep with plans of food on our lips—"Flan de coco or arroz con leche?" I mumble. "Yes, of course we can make an *ajiaco*. . . ." The food-shaped words float between us. We press them between our bodies and are satisfied.

Fidel

In the third week of his visit, Alejandro finally refers to "him" directly—he saw "him" once. It was 1975, and Alejandro was studying at the university when Fidel Castro paid a surprise visit. Alejandro was standing with a group of students when Fidel singled him out and asked how his studies were going. Until this point whenever we've talked about politics, Alejandro has referred to institutions—the government, the state, the people, the ministry of this or that—a labyrinth of work groups, organizations, committees, ministries, centers, and bureaucracies that all silently and unequivocally lead to one man.

"What was he like?"

"Fidel had a large presence, an enormous presence—the whole thing made me nervous."

This is the only time Alejandro refers to "him" by name. Usually he calls Castro *el presidente*. It's as if the people of Cuba have swallowed his name and integrated the figure so wholly that to articulate it would be redundant. I imagine what it's like to be surrounded by Fidel—his wants, needs, vision, and demands—but hardly ever to speak his name. Cubans mostly refer to him using gestures. They tug at an imaginary beard or cross their right hand over their chest and tap three fingers on the left shoulder to indicate military stripes. If they speak of him, they call him the Leader, the Commander, the Boss, or my favorite, *ya tú sabes* (you know who).

We walk the streets of Bogotá, talking endlessly of Cuba and the United States, socialism and capitalism, imperialism and art. Alejandro squeezes my hand. He always places himself on the outside of the sidewalk, closest to the traffic. Returning from Carulla one afternoon, he mentions he used to go to the theater all the time. He says his wife would go too. I bristle. We haven't discussed his wife since I was in Cuba. Despite the pang of anxiety reverberating in me, a warning sounds in my head to let him talk about her. A bus sweeps by with some kids hanging off the back end, and Alejandro, still not used to so much traffic, steers me to the inside of the sidewalk and pauses, looking over his shoulder at the street. We resume walking.

"At first she went to everything," he explains, still looking over his shoulder at the lumbering stream of traffic behind us. "Over time, she stayed home more and more. Then the Special Period came and no one went anywhere. I think that's when I realized that we'd completely grown apart." Alejandro looks at the sidewalk in front of him as he says this. I, too, look at the sidewalk. For the first time, I wonder if his marriage fell apart on its own, as marriages do, or if its demise was the result of the decaying social structures. The fall of the Berlin Wall, the dismantling of the Soviet Union, the end of the USSR's economic support that sustained Cuba, and the decay of Alejandro's marriage. How did these events affect one another? I'm curious about the connection, but I don't ask. The end of a lifelong commitment, the extinction of a political system—no ending can fully explain the twining of these plots and subplots.

A Cuban from the island. An American of Cuban descent. We're completely removed from our families, our friends, and our professional and personal concerns. We spend one month feeding each other, telling stories about what our lives were like before we met. We try to better understand each other's country, and we dance. We dance.

On any given late afternoon or evening, salsa blares from the windows and doors of Bogotá's Laundromats, kiosks, bars, and clubs. The Monday after Alejandro arrives, we walk around La Zona Rosa, an upscale neighborhood of bars and restaurants close to my apartment. We see a lovely cobblestone patio with hanging plants, but it's too cold to sit outside, so we enter the bar. The bartender is chatting with a few regulars and popping CDs in and out of the stereo. He puts on Ricardo Lemvo, an African-born, Los Angeles–based salsa musician I've been listening to lately. The single "Mambo Yo-Yo" pulsates from the speakers, and we rush to the floor without even taking off our coats.

After a few more songs, the DJ plays a Rubén Blades' classic, "Pedro Navaja," an ode to death, violence, and New York City. Alejandro grabs my hand and squeezes my waist as a scattered group of dancers makes their way to the floor. He spins me around him in circle after circle, whirling me into Blades' wise refrain, "La vida te da sorpresa, sorpresa te da la vida." The dark irony of Blades' lilting "I like to live in America" scrapes between us, and we burst out laughing.

For this month, I live out my desire to dance. We enter bars and go directly to the dance floor, forgetting to take off our coats and uninterested in ordering drinks. We insert ourselves into the music: we squeeze between the long-throated trombone and furious percussion. The more we talk about our countries and their long history, the more we acknowledge it through dance. We dance with the same enthusiasm to expatriate songstress Celia Cruz, long ago erased from Cuba's musical canon, as we do Cuba's famed Iraquere or Los Van Van. I'm awestruck when Alejandro confesses only a vague recognition of Cruz's name and no knowledge at all of several Cuban musicians, now exiles, who have been completely "erased" by the government.

But Miami also has its history of musical repression. Although they are not officially banned and can be heard on radio stations throughout the United States, Los Van Van are never heard on Miami's airwaves. In 1999, when the group played its first concert in Miami, concertgoers were met with bottle-throwing protestors and police in riot gear. Even the Little Havana bar Hoy Como Ayer (formerly the legendary Café Nostalgia that Zoé Valdés wrote about in her novel of the same title) has received numerous threats for letting acts from the island play on its stage. As we share stories and dance, we quietly dedicate ourselves to dancing to all kinds of music, to moving within music both revolutionary and prerevolutionary, both American and Cuban. I think Alejandro and I can transform history, just a little, through dance.

I'd thought this time with Alejandro would help me finally understand Cuba. I'd thought I'd come to some conclusions. In fact I do, but not the ones I'd imagined. Despite thinking of myself as "open-minded," I realize how deeply I want Cuba to be unequivocally "bad" or "good." I want conversations like the following to end with the point I believe is true:

"But there are no free elections. That's the main characteristic of a dictatorship," I assert.

"Yes, there are elections. The people have voted for the current president," Alejandro replies.

"But the people aren't given any other options, so that's not a free election."

"Anyone can run for president of Cuba."

As a member of a university think tank, Alejandro and his work fall undeniably under the domain of the government; but because it's his job to analyze the human condition of the people around him, he can't just pretend everything is okay. He admits Cuba's longtime economic dependency on the Soviet Union was a dire mistake. He speaks of the 1989 trial and execution by firing squad of General Arnaldo Ochoa as a terrifying moment in recent history. He also was old enough to remember the rancor that broke out amongst neighbors during the Mariel Boatlift, those who were committed to the Revolution lashing out at those who were fleeing the country.

"There's a tremendous amount of envy and pressure emerging now," Alejandro explains. "Some people have family in the States and others don't. There's a great resentment and a growing divide between those who receive economic support and those who must suffer without it." He goes on to confirm what I've suspected: that a color line exists between the "haves" and "have-nots." Black Cubans are less likely to have family members in the States, so they receive less support from abroad. I wonder which side of the color line Alejandro falls on: he is not black, but with his honey-colored complexion, he's definitely not white either. I ask Alejandro, and he says he considers himself too mixed to call himself either white or black, and that besides a priest in St. Paul, Minnesota, he has no family in the States.

We construct a loose box of salsa around ourselves. Working in small squares, we build a space where we can be humorous, tender, quiet, or expansive. It's the first space we inhabit together. Alejandro dips me into a deep back bend. We spin, laugh, and turn. We dance at home—in the hallway, the kitchen. We turn on music and spin around the living room floor, stepping over the newspapers and shoes scattered there. He dips me again and jokingly pretends to drop me. We turn into each other, walk away, then face each other again without missing a beat.

I learn that moving in unison has nothing to do with anticipating my partner's moves. To the contrary, when I concentrate on listening to the music—when the chorus reaches its crescendo or a steady beat switches tempo—if I simply listen to that, when I pivot on one foot and turn, Alejandro will be there. Language enters through my ears and mouth, but dance is more magical. Its beats and rhythms pass through impenetrable skin and bones. We dance early in the morning before going to the university, and I step into the brisk air heady and flushed.

Months later, people will come up to me at Son Salomé, a local bar near the university, and say, "Hey, I saw you in that club on the other side of town" or "I saw you downtown. You were dancing like crazy with a short morenito." Months later, it will seem that all of Bogotá witnessed Alejandro and me falling in love. I imagine we will marry; we'll live in a third country together, writing and dancing. With Alejandro, the world will be a better place. With him, anything can be done.

Family Album

"Perhaps he's too tender," Alejandro worries. I look at the picture of his son, who has dark eyes unfolding like wings.

"Of course he's too tender."

There's a brand of boy like this—one whose huge doe eyes must negotiate with an average, even homely, face. Alejandro is showing me photos of his boy looking up from a large, imposing table, his girl with her friends.

"They look like American kids," I say, referring to Alejandro's daughter and her friends, striking rapper poses in oversized jeans and tight Tommy T-shirts.

It's a Sunday afternoon and we've just been to a small movie house in Chapinero Alto. Afterwards, we stroll down a tree-lined street past German-style apartments constructed from brick, with wooden lattices and Swiss flower boxes in the windowsills. Soon, we stop in an outdoor café. Alejandro has carried the photo album under his arm all afternoon, never explaining its presence or asking me if I'd like to look at it. I'm getting used to his strange way of possessing things. A head of lettuce clutched in one hand, a family album pinned silently under his arm—he holds each object so deliberately it seems to separate from him and, in turn, take on a presence of its own. Simple objects, framed in his absence, gather the meaning and import of a still-life painting, and so it is with the red glossy photo album before us.

Two lush elms sway overhead, shushing each other. The sun has emerged from behind Bogotá's clouds and smog, giving the illusion of a golden autumn afternoon. Alejandro looks at me expectantly before he turns each page, as if he doesn't know what's coming next. After examining each photo, I nod for him to proceed, and he carefully folds over the next page. I compliment his son's incredible eyes, his daughter's beauty. I ask how they manage to feed the scrappy dog wagging its tail in the corner of one of the photos. I nod, the page turns, and finally, the family photo appears. I take in a sharp breath, a silent gasp. We both stare at the picture of Alejandro, his wife, and his two children.

"What do you think?" he asks.

"Well, there you all are," I observe, forcing myself to keep my eyes on the photo. Is he touching her? Does he seem distant? I notice the woman looks older than me, that she is older, as is Alejandro. While I was studying for finals in college, they were building a family. In fact, they look like a family, a real unit. I break eye contact with the photo and look up at him.

"I don't know what to think." I wonder why he has shown me this picture, the family photo: to prove to me that he has a family? To remind himself? To get his wife and me in the same room? To be honest? To lie?

Alejandro closes the album and begins to clear a space for the waiter who's brought guava pastry and a slice of pear tart with a drizzle of *arequipe*, Colombia's version of *dulce de leche*. A couple with light woolen scarves draped around their necks arrives and sits at the table next to us.

"I needed you to see this," Alejandro smiles, nodding at the album, now sitting obediently at his side. He puts his hand on mine and sticks a fork into the pastry, offering me a bite before taking one himself. He thinks the moment has passed and that we're now on to something else, but I am still reeling from the family photo.

It's one thing to know about his family and another thing to see him with them. I stare at the couple next to us, casually scanning the menu and chatting. The man's hair is a bit mussed and his dark chocolate-colored scarf droops casually, giving him a distracted, intellectual air. The woman's scarf falls in two wide ribbons down her back. Their understated style connects them effortlessly. I look from Alejandro's family photo to this couple ordering tea. In one moment, I lose him. I send Alejandro back to his wife and ration book, his children, and the big house leaking at the corners, rotting at the foundation.

Until now, love has been the answer to all my questions and doubts, but in one moment, these new images incorporate themselves into our story and alter it in a way love can't refute. Alejandro's family tree is firmly planted and verdant. If I betray his wife and children, I betray him, because they are part of his body. If I hurt them, I'm hurting him. They are born of him, cut from his side, leaflike and sprawling. In one moment, I remember the name of one flower and forgot the name of another. Our story is like that.

"You know what? All talk of 'us' is at best bad luck and at worst doomed," I state flatly, referring to the increasing number of discussions we've been having about our future together. My voice sounds detached, as if I'm repeating a line from a movie.

Alejandro puts down his fork and considers what I have to say. Even in the moments when most men would sigh and think, "Jesus, here we go," Alejandro is completely present.

"I've had a revelation," I declare. "After all the conversations, analyses, pledges, and declarations of love, I've had one crystalline moment." I say this knowing that it belittles our conversations, but I feel punchy and belligerent, drunk almost.

Alejandro gives me an encouraging nod.

"Nothing right can come from something wrong." I parade my cliché shamelessly.

Alejandro's hands are resting on the table. He gently interlocks his fingers and leans toward me.

"*This*," I gesture back and forth across the space between us, "is wrong." I take a deep breath and continue, "You have a wife. You have children. We shouldn't be here. Nothing good can come from this."

He smiles at me fondly, almost patronizingly.

"In fact," I add, waving my finger in giddy emphasis, "If I love you, how could I hurt your loved ones?"

"I don't think *this* is something wrong," Alejandro says in a calm, rational tone, as if he's already thought it through. "I don't think loving someone is a bad thing, and while I recognize the moral ramifications of hurting others, I think we can find a way to make. . . ."

"Wait. You're a philosopher, right?" I interrupt in an accusing tone. "Isn't there some logical fallacy that falls under trying to make something right out of something wrong? You know, post hoc, ergo propter hoc, or something like that?"

I leave the dessert and the scarved couple, stirring their tea absentmindedly. I leave Alejandro, who quickly stands up and trails behind me. I'm growing cold, all of my emotions settling into their various compartments, crackling and freezing like cubes in a metal ice tray. Alejandro catches up and walks beside me in silence. He turns to me at a stoplight and says, "Please say something." But I'm cold. My anger, sadness, and guilt are set in their little trays and hardening. Mentally, I place him in the past tense, *I fell in love with a Cuban I met in Bogotá.* Although my heart still thinks of him in the present tense of finite pleasures—the brown lily of his sex, the way he hums absentmindedly while eating—I will him into the past tense. I imagine myself back in Miami, sitting around a carafe of Merlot with a few close friends and confiding, "I was crazy about him," then the irresistible sarcasm . . . "or maybe I was just crazy." I hear my mother's cavalier tone creeping in.

The light turns green, and Alejandro wraps his hand gently around my arm to prevent me from walking away. "I had no idea the album would upset you so much. I should have shown it to you somewhere more private."

"Can I tell you a story about my mother?" I blurt out.

"Okay," he smiles uneasily and steers me toward a concrete stoop in front of a tall, glass apartment building.

"Every story my mother ever told me about my birth was a joke," I say.

Alejandro looks confused.

"I mean it was told in the form of a joke, with that tone," I try to clarify, realizing that the word *joke* is too literal.

His brow furrows in concentration and he leans in closer as if he's not hearing me clearly. I tell him what my mother always told me: that she didn't realize she was pregnant until she was six months along. According to my mother, when the doctor told her she was going to have a baby, he asked her incredulously, "You're a nurse. Didn't you feel it kicking?" and my mother replied in her cavalier tone, "I thought it was gas." She arrived at the hospital to give birth wearing three-inch stiletto heels, a pencil skirt, and freshly manicured nails. The admitting nurse gave her a long look and replied, "Lady, I look more pregnant than you do." In the delivery room, she refused a pillow because it would have messed up the platinum blonde beehive piled atop her head. She always bragged about dropping below her pre-pregnancy weight once she'd given birth. "I'd always weighed 126," she boasted. "The day I had you, I weighed 133. After I gave birth, I weighed 125. I'd lost one pound and you!" she joked. My mother punctuated every piece of the story with a punch line until the very end when the doctor announced, "It's a baby girl" and my mother replied, "Whoops! I forgot to take my pill."

I find it almost impossible to translate all of this to Alejandro. It's not a lack of vocabulary. The words are simple: *pill, doctor, baby*. It's the humor. How to translate my mother's unbridled sarcasm toward my birth without making her sound cruel or unnatural. Even though many pregnancy stories have a slapstick quality to them—a journey to the hospital that rivals the Keystone Cops, or the string of obscenities a mother utters at the height of contractions—my mother's sardonic attitude toward my birth has always had a different tone—one I now find utterly impossible to communicate to Alejandro until I state one simple fact: "My mother was alone when she gave birth. There were no friends or family present."

His face finally registers understanding. "That must have been so difficult."

"I always hated it when my mother repeated these stories," I tell Alejandro, who's been listening attentively, an occasional puzzled look flashing across his face. I don't tell him how I learned to cut my mother off when I was older. I'd roll my eyes and snap that I'd heard the story and she was repeating herself. Sometimes I even parroted her own punch line to shut her up. But as a child, I was incapable of fending off these stories that made my stomach churn with anxiety, so I'd curl into a small place inside of myself.

I felt angry and bewildered, unsure why the stories made me so uncomfortable. I'd always thought my mother's humor and nonchalant attitude hurt because of the obvious—no kid wants to think of him- or herself as an accident. But today, here with Alejandro and his family album, I'd stumbled upon the pain roiling below the surface—my mother's absolute loneliness and isolation, the loneliness she communicated in her jokes, her pain of being a mother and father to me, with no family to support her.

"Today, for the first time since I met you, I feel alone in the same way I felt when my mother used to tell those stories. I feel alone in the way I imagine she felt," I tell Alejandro.

He looks surprised and slightly hurt, but I continue.

"I don't want us to become some story I tell ten years from now. I don't want us to become some joke I have to make to keep from falling apart."

He pulls me close and I start to sob into the sleeve of his insulated jacket. Cars pass, a dog hobbles by, and still I cry. I try to let out the tears and let go of this strange memory of my mother that has surfaced, but I can't. Despite the geographical distance between us, I am haunted by my mother and her stories. Why was she alone? Why did she keep me such a secret, even from her family?

"I feel scared too," Alejandro says. "Your mother was a very brave person to have you like that. Maybe you fear we're not that brave."

"Maybe I don't want to be that brave," I reply. He wraps his arms around me and we get up and continue walking home. At the end of my mother's bravado and feisty storytelling is me—the person she sacrificed for, the person she raised alone. I don't want to bear that burden for anyone or have anyone else bear such a weight for me.

We walk along the sidewalk, past the Carulla where we've bought so much fruit, cheese, and bread over the last few weeks. The carts rattle and individuals hawk *arepas*, fresh juices, and newspapers from improvised kiosks.

This morning, I discovered a startling birthmark on Alejandro's chest: a cherry-colored mole identical to the one my mother has on her neck. It's the delicate, deep pink color one would expect to find on a fair-skinned, freckled complexion. Only my mother, in her rapture and rancor, could have placed it there. She placed it there for me to recognize love as something misplaced, an anomaly.

We walk in silence. We pass a large Catholic church. I raise my hand and make the sign of the cross, a habit I've picked up from the Bogotanos. I'm not a practicing Catholic but I am an ardent ritualist. I'm captivated by the way a simple gesture can imbue the most mundane daily action with reverence. The plaza in front of the church holds a bustling Sunday market. Women sit at black felt tables, each one stocked with innumerable variations of the one thing being sold there. If the table displays stockings, it offers endless colors, textures, styles, and so on.

The sun is setting behind the large stone church and its granite plaza. I think of Mary Magdalene, discovering Jesus in a crowded market like this one or dining at a rich man's home, how she fell to her knees, unfastened her hair, and wept, washing his feet with her tears. Having been known as a prostitute, she showed great courage to kneel before a man in public like that. The message of Christ is that we all have something of God in us, but Mary Magdalene knew this. She didn't need Christ to be a miracle worker, magician, or healer. She needed him to be a man. He had a limp, he had a bad foot. He smelled of a bitter root. She reached into his robes and pulled out a flute that produced a whimsical melody with a raspy, sorrowful undertone that called the heavenly notes back down to the earth. Not a savior or prophet, but a man, flesh enveloping a divine tune.

Jesus' message was that we all possess divine essence. Magdalena's lesson is that the divine exists because of the flesh. She fell to her knees not to be forgiven or to become respected in the community. She knelt to give thanks. With the same gesture, I give thanks. After all the flesh, Alejandro is flesh. After all the betrayal, Alejandro too is betrayal. After all the solitude—in him, with him, I'm still alone.

Out of the corner of my eye, I watch Alejandro, with his carefully buttoned shirt and efficiently arranged family album. He has conceived and reared children. He has loved and experienced birth. I haven't, so I can only give him my fluids, swallow into him my idiosyncrasies—my irrational arms winding, my cloud heart darkening. Metaphor. I can give him comparisons, approximations, but to talk of love in a concrete way is a violation I don't wish to commit, an insult against his wife, the woman who has shared him with the earth generously, patiently for all these years, letting him go off to think, write, and look for food. Or maybe she hasn't been generous. Maybe she's been greedy, keeping him to herself but ignoring him. Aren't all marriages created and destroyed on basic principles of generosity? I don't praise her. I don't condemn her. We can't rob each other.

We will not compete to "win" him. I'm resolved and grateful for this. What a burden—to win him, to capture or catch him. One thing is certain: neither of us will ever have all of him. There are parts of him that he will never extract from her and parts that he'll never relinquish to me. Like any animal in a forest, he'll finally choose to wander in one direction or another based on instinct, based on the highest promise of comfort, food, and shelter. But unlike an animal, he'll carry with him the knowledge that in choosing one thing, he loses another, something that can never be recuperated. Unlike an animal, he will miss what he hasn't chosen. He'll suffer for it.

As I'm unlocking the door to the apartment, Alejandro grabs my elbow, "Don't ever shut me out like this again. Please."

I turn to him and ask the mundane, the inevitable: "Don't you feel bad?" We go inside and collapse on the overstuffed couch. My bag falls heavily to my side.

"I feel bad for my kids," Alejandro considers. "Bad that we didn't end our marriage before it got to this point." He turns toward me and considers his words, "But no, I don't feel bad about being with you, about being in love, because it's sincere. Just as every failed attempt at making my wife happy, at making our marriage work, has been sincere, so I guess I feel destiny brought me to this moment."

"Destiny from an atheist?" I tease. "A Marxist sense of destiny? Does this include the masses?"

"How can it not?"

"Destiny for the people, hmmm." I consider. "Historically, that's always ended badly."

"History is a dialectic," he offers gamely. "It's always in motion."

We brew chamomile tea. We're both exhausted, too tired to make a fire, so we arrange ourselves under a pile of blankets and wrap our hands around the steaming mugs. The sun has gone down. I don't know when. The fireplace is dark, but there are some lights on at the end of the hall. In the less than half light, I notice the asymmetry of his features, his warm eyes, his molten lower lip.

He looks at me annoyed, upset that I could detach from him so completely, perhaps relieved that we are talking again. He lets out an exasperated sigh and pulls me toward him. Alejandro's heart is still tender after so many years of revolution, hunger, and failure, and I wonder how it has stayed so. I notice he's getting old. His skin is wrinkled and creased. Like a rock, he's been thrown around part of the time, neglected under the base of a house the rest. Like a stone, he remains solemn, self-contained, but still thirsty, just a few inches from the sea.

I call him Eve and he wraps himself around me, winds up my leg. I call him Evening and he says, "It's late. I'm tired." He wants us to lie down and rest. I take his hand and agree. It's time to rest, and for this one night, one of the last ones before he returns to Cuba, nothing touches our lips, not even water. We lie in the dark and sleep and tickle and move inside each other. We rest and sleep and converse into the hour, speaking into it like children into a seashell—fascinated, excited, unburdened by time.

Storm

Alejandro is stranded. He's a castaway on an island that exports castaways. He travels to Central America, South America, and Africa, where he humbly but firmly expounds the anti-imperialist lectures he's written with his work group. His speeches have such titles as "The Sham of Globalization" and "Modern-Day Peasants in the New Age of Imperialism."

On these trips, his leftist friends take up collections to give him dollars and buy him food, clothes, electronic equipment—whatever he can haul back to Cuba. In exchange, Alejandro gives them the moral high ground. He criticizes the status quo of the American cow: the bigger it gets, the more it eats, and it's eating up the rest of the world. In the meantime, he hoards sandals for his daughter, shampoos and lipsticks for his wife, a puzzle for his son, and lots of dried food and nonperishable goods. The irony doesn't make it into Alejandro's lectures, but he's not oblivious to it either. He worries that ideologies have become so polarized that no middle ground exists where regular people can thrive.

I hurl his duffel bag of goods onto the conveyer belt. He pats the bulging canvas form and stares after it with a parent's worried expression. Beforehand, we'd agreed on a very brief goodbye, and to my relief Alejandro honors that and doesn't linger. After a few waves, he vanishes around a corner and disappears inside the gate. Alejandro's gone, and I'm glowing with the idea that we'll be together. The wife doesn't want him. She tired of their marriage long ago. Surely, she'll be relieved to let him go. And Cuba eagerly rents him out to other countries. It's to her advantage to do so. An intellectual's antiglobalization message sounds quite rational and convincing in contrast to the image of Fidel ranting and raving in army fatigues and designer tennis shoes. So undoubtedly, the wife will let me have Alejandro, and Cuba will dispatch him to some unidentified third world country where I can collect him and his lightweight duffel bag at the airport. These are the thoughts that cycle through my brain in the first couple of weeks after Alejandro's departure, keeping me cheerful and detached, like a low-dose antidepressant.

Alejandro sends an e-mail, and we agree on a time for me to call him. After a few tries, the call finally goes through. He gets on the phone and explains that the island has been hit by a tropical storm. There's a steady beeping in the background, and even worse, an echo. The last few words of each sentence ricochet between us, so we each must pause before responding to let the other's sentence reverberate in the receiver. At first we laugh, but the echo quickly becomes distracting and annoying.

"Are you okay?" I enunciate carefully into the receiver, holding it out like a microphone.

"Yes. I miss you," a faint, slightly gargled voice materializes on the other end.

It's been two weeks now, and I'm tense, wondering what's happening. I know Alejandro was going to talk to his wife, and I want to be able to understand everything clearly.

"Let's wait for the storm to pass. I can call you in a couple of days," I suggest, but Alejandro interjects a "No" into my "días." As "No" echoes over the Caribbean to Cuba and boomerangs back to my three-story, brick apartment building in Bogotá, he repeats, "No, we need to talk now," in an uncharacteristically firm voice. He has resumed *relaciones* with his wife.

When he told her he wanted a divorce, she pulled herself together as never before and begged him to let her try to save the marriage. She's set out to listen and talk, to pay attention to him in a way she hasn't for years. Alejandro's wife did everything opposite from what he'd expected. She's making a complete metamorphosis. He relates all of this in a neutral tone except for a slight edge to his voice that seems to plead, "Try to understand. I have no other alternative here." In fact, he does say, "How could I not give her one chance after so many years of marriage?"

The "what" of English could be easily misinterpreted here. If I say "Qué?" he might simply repeat what he just said more slowly, thinking I didn't understand him. I opt for the javelin that will ask for an explanation while confirming I understand everything he just said:

"Cómo?" I cast it toward the Caribbean, knowing it will hit its mark even though the effort is ultimately useless. "Cómo?" I repeat in disbelief. *How?* How could you? How could this be? I slide down the wall and sit with my knees pressed to my chest. My chest caves in as I curl rigidly around the phone, bracing myself for grief. My whole body has become one alert, expectant human ear.

"Yo sé," Alejandro sighs. He *knows*? With the reverberation of the phone line, his *sé* sounds more like "say." What does he know? What is he going to say? Before he can continue, his long, jagged "saaay" begins to crackle. I hold the phone out. The static sputters and hisses for several seconds, then the line goes completely dead. Still clutching the receiver, I stare through the window at the apartment buildings next to mine. Bogotá remains hard and damp outdoors, the sky gray and cold, while Alejandro's world is being seized by high-force winds and squalls, palm leaves thrashing and whipping at the buildings.

I had thought myself the woman and he the man. I'd thought myself the harbor and he the wrecked ship that would soon be delivered to my safety. I would welcome him, envelop him, make him whole again. Suddenly, I realize I'm the potentially destructive force. I'm the impending catastrophe that's whirled into Alejandro's life and startled his wife into action. I'm the storm that's set her into motion: she's taking inventory, cleaning house, battening down the hatches, nailing loose objects to the ground, trying to keep her home intact. *Yo sé*. Does he really think I can commiserate? Is there anything else we can know or say? Both verbs feel equally impotent and ridiculous.

In Bogotá, Alejandro and I went over and over his relationship—the long trajectory, the distance, and ultimately, the fundamental differences between him and his wife. She is the one who would have been happy leaving for Miami to earn more money. She removed herself from their bed. She no longer wanted to go to the theater or ballet.

Suddenly, she is someone else. How can one woman transform another from a profoundly unhappy spouse to a jealous wife who will do anything to save her marriage? My father's wife could answer this question. The day my mother called and asked to speak with my father, Zoraida's reluctant concession that she would allow him to get to know his long-lost daughter changed dramatically.

It's late May 1988, and I'm visiting my father a second time. The exhilaration and headiness from the newness of our first visit has worn off. Zoraida's harboring a quiet rage—one that only another woman or a husband of many years could detect. My father buys me a pair of shoes, Zoraida insists on a new coat. I say maybe I'd like to live in Miami someday. Zoraida says they are planning to move to Puerto Rico. Still, things seem manageable. I make sure I chat mostly with her. I compliment her cooking and ask her which blouse goes best with my linen skirt. She is civil to me, but cold. Occasionally, she is gregarious despite herself. Nevertheless, a sense of impending doom slowly clamps down on my stomach. Finally, Zoraida's rage and my sense of doom catalyze on May 25, when my mother calls and asks to speak to José, to whom she announces that it's my birthday. My father mutters a few reserved, cordial words into the phone and hands it to me.

I can imagine my mother on the other end, propped up on a mound of pillows in bed or on the couch, watching *Wheel of Fortune*, sentries of medicine vials and a tall glass of heavily iced diet Coke at her side. My mother was a nurse from the old school: she believed in pills to pick you up and pills to put you to sleep.

"Happy Birthday, Baby," her voice gurgles as if underwater. In twenty years my parents have not spoken, and I never imagined that when they finally did speak, I'd be on my father's end of the phone. I'm standing at the kitchen bar where we eat all our meals. Cabinet doors slam, plates and glasses rattle. Zoraida's Spanish flies like a thousand black wings scattered by a single shot. I cringe. She's furious that my mother has called and that she's asked to speak with my father. The moment feels irreversible and catastrophic.

I return to Missouri. Several months later, at Christmastime, I receive a card signed by both of them in Zoraida's hand, then nothing. When I call, she pretends he's not home. When I call, she pretends she doesn't understand me or that I have the wrong number or she simply hangs up. I can bring myself to do this only a few times, with several months between each call, enough time for me to persuade myself that maybe she really didn't recognize my voice or there must have been some kind of mistake. But each time, I'll check and double-check directory assistance. Each time, her sharp "Oigo" and the click of the receiver will confirm her identity and the reality that I'll never manage to get through. One year after that two-minute phone call, all communication with my father has been completely severed.

In the days that follow the conversation with Alejandro, I spend my lunch money on taxis. I collapse into their backseats, grateful to be carted around. I hesitate before exiting, then walk briskly to my office and my classroom, refusing leaflets and denying beggars with a terse wave of the hand. I can't bear to be around people. Ensconced within the glass walls of the office I share with several other professors, I compulsively check for e-mails and feel alternately angry and relieved when the ".cu" extension doesn't appear on the screen.

All the while, the word *relaciones* has broken off like a spore and multiplied in my imagination. That's the word Alejandro used, and although I've never heard it before in this particular context, it has entered my consciousness with a thrust of meaning. One afternoon before my class, I'm alone in the office, and although I fight the urge, I finally can't resist. I take a Spanish-English dictionary from the shelf. A part of me I have no control over is harboring the fantasy that in English, *relaciones* might have some meaning I don't know. Perhaps Alejandro has established a relationship with his wife where they can be honest and evaluate their marriage sensibly. Perhaps they can become good friends. It's true. The first definition I come across refers to relationships and being on good terms with other human beings. Then there's the angle of business connections and contacts and finally, the context of diplomatic relations and *relaciones exteriores*—foreign affairs. Starkly situated among these definitions, is the meaning "Sex."

I fall into the habit of arriving in my office, slouching over my desk, and sobbing before I go to class. One day, Inez, one of my office mates, places a cold, heavily ringed hand on my shoulder. She comes from an old, wealthy Bogotá family and has been married for thirty-two years. After a few moments of silence, she removes her hand and says, "I've been there." Walking away, she calls over her shoulder, "On the other side, but I've been there."

Another coworker puts her hand on my shoulder, then another. Marisa is still single and lives with her mother, who's partially paralyzed and needs round-the-clock care. Carlota had her son at fifteen years of age. They live in a converted apartment behind her parents' house, a two-hour commute from the university. They've all "been there," but the cool, jeweled hands that press into my back extend neither sympathy nor wisdom. My coworkers keep their distance, knowing that my pain could easily ignite their own sadness or fury, whichever "side" of the triangle they've been on. The offerings of clean tissues and warm cocoa placed silently by my side tell me this is an epidemic and, if I survive it, a rite of passage.

Stone

Three weeks later, a few days before Christmas, I'm back in Cuba. While Alejandro was in Bogotá, I bought a nonrefundable ticket to Havana. Did I really have that much faith that everything would work out, or was I trying to convince myself? At this point, I have no idea, but I do know that my goal in working and saving in Bogotá was to go to Cuba, and this is my last chance before returning to the States, so uncertain but obstinate, I trudge forward with my plans.

Alejandro finds me hefting my luggage onto a shiny new cart at the José Martí International Airport. He's carefully holding a single, tired rose, its pink bud closed tightly, the edges tinged with an institutional yellow. Alejandro's expression is equally tired. He looks older, and I smile to myself wryly, thinking this would be the most predictable scene in a bad novel—the young heroine realizes that her older lover is indeed older. This is just the kind of ending that was in my heart all along, nagging me.

Along with the rational voice insisting the relationship with Alejandro was foolish, a cliché flickers in my mind's eye like a B movie one halfheartedly watches while doing something else: young woman, but in her early thirties (not so young)—time to have an affair with a married man. No, worse, time to fall in love with a married man. Truth exists in that cliché, but facing Alejandro's nervous presence before me, I realize my self-mocking is an attempt to suppress a more painful reality: I love him. He doesn't give me a meaningful hug or try to kiss me. Instead he's warm, capable and, to me, he's beautiful with his weathered skin, muscular forearms, and closely cropped, graying hair.

Flights from Mexico City, the Bahamas, and Jamaica are pouring into the airport. Families are roped off at the entrance. They wait by the dozens, anxiously clutching the rope. As soon as their loved ones come through immigration, they cry out, embrace them, and sweep them away. There's no hanging out at the airport, "congregating" as the Cuban officials would call it, which makes for the speediest airport reunions I've ever seen.

Amidst all of the confusion, I wonder for a brief moment if there was a mistake. Maybe the conversation where Alejandro told me he had "resumed relaciones" with his wife never really took place. Maybe he's here, like everyone else, to cry, embrace, and whisk his loved one off to Havana. As if on cue, Alejandro looks over and hugs me spontaneously, "I'm so happy to see you," he whispers in my ear, sending a chill across my neck, but when he pulls away, I see his eyes are red, and despite his effort to appear cheerful, he's sad and tired.

We file out of the airport, and within a couple of minutes, we're in a private taxi rattling toward Havana with all the windows down. He tells me there's been a change of plans and I can't stay at Niurka's. "She's in the hospital," he says, explaining that Niurka had some kind of nervous breakdown and has been hospitalized for the last couple of months. "I didn't want to tell you about it until I could see her for myself and get a handle on the situation."

"Did you see her?"

His eyes signal in the direction of the cab driver, and he says, "More on that later"—several days later, as it turns out. I can't imagine why a cab driver would find Niurka's breakdown interesting or significant, but in Cuba although the silent nods and often unfulfilled promises of explanations aren't clear, one message is: don't trust anyone, and this seems doubly true for cab drivers—the official and unofficial ones alike. Alejandro settles in for the ride and turns to me, pointing at the rose that I had forgotten I'm still holding, "Read what it says," he urges, his voice tinged with impatient excitement. He'd wrapped a thin, rectangular piece of computer paper around the stem and secured it with a sliver of clear tape. The message in italicized print reads, "I will always love you."

I smile, focusing on the craftsmanship not the message, "So it looks like you guys finally got a printer in your office, huh?" He nods enthusiastically and adds, "I did it myself. It took me over an hour to print it out correctly." He goes on to tell me that, initially at least, I'll be staying with Niurka's parents, who have a bed and breakfast (certified with the state and everything) in a neighborhood called Nuevo Vedado.

"They're going to give you a discount because you're Niurka's friend," he continues, adding that his work group would like to get together with me and have a *tertulia*, an informal gathering to converse, read poetry, and listen to music.

"These last few months, they've put as much faith in us as I have," he smiles wistfully. "They're really anxious to meet you." He also lists some things I might be interested in doing—going to a concert in a recently restored Havana cathedral, seeing a play that might be opening, visiting some people he knows who can put me in touch with young Cuban poets to interview.

We arrive at Nuevo Vedado, where Niurka's stepfather, Eddy, and her mother, Linda, live. The expansive, art-deco homes from the fifties indicate that this was once an upper-middle-class neighborhood. Eddy and Linda belong to the class of Cubans who were part of the prerevolutionary bourgeoisie but chose to ally themselves with Castro and are now a silent, virtually inactive component of the Cuban old guard. On my previous trip, I'd noticed a photo of Fidel Castro at Niurka's parents' wedding. "No one knows why," Niurka told me with a silent, knowing glance, "but my father shot himself in the head a few years after the Revolution." Linda then married Eddy. Together, they rent rooms from their two-story house, which they call a bed and breakfast.

Linda and Eddy's living room is decorated with china, a divan, and little porcelain figures from the fifties, some in black face. In the garage, Eddy has three refrigerators, none of them in working condition, where he stores *mamey*, *fruta bomba*, and mango, which he mashes into a baby-food-like substance that he tries to push off on me in the mornings for breakfast. Eddy pays the government fees and licenses to keep his place legal, but he sometimes takes in people like me, charges them less than the going rate, and doesn't report the income. Mainly, he and Linda rely on their son who's a chef in France and sends them money regularly.

Over the next couple of days, I realize that Linda is one of the many reborn Catholics swept up by the revitalization of the Catholic Church that occurred in 1998 when the pope made his historic visit to Cuba. While dusting off her mammy doll figurines in the sitting room or shelving various-sized jars of purée with Eddy in the garage, she often looks distracted, and she frequently removes a neatly folded piece of paper from the pocket of her flowered housedress and mutters the tail end of a Bible verse or prayer. Sometimes I see Linda take a little white tablet from her apron and swallow it without water. "Tranquilizers," my friend Odalys will later explain. "They give them to everyone."

As I quickly throw my bags in the upstairs room and splash some water on my face, I hear Eddy and Alejandro having a conversation that sounds amicable but a bit forced. In the eyes of the average Cuban, Alejandro is not simply a philosopher and researcher. He's part of the system. Every branch of education and research leads to the government, so Eddy and Linda treat him with the respect and cautiousness reserved for civil servants.

Alejandro and I eat fried chicken at a corner snack bar a couple of blocks from the house. The stone wings and giant mausoleums of the Cementerio Colón, Havana's largest cemetery, are just across the street, silent and beautiful. The sun is starting to set, and I'm anxious to walk around. Alejandro and I step into the night, holding hands. We walk into long stretches of silence and darkness. The road winds, dips, and curves, but we're always moving forward. As we pass through gradations of darkness, the stone walls of the cemetery emit coolness.

We follow a narrow, gravelly path behind buildings and houses, brushing back tree branches with our arms. We hear a sound up ahead: a crackly radio, then the brassiness of contemporary salsa with a bit of hip-hop and a pelvis-grinding bass beat. The road opens into a large street, and we come upon several couples dancing *la rueda de casino*. Someone calls out the moves with the speed and efficiency of an auctioneer, while couples fluidly spin, lunge, shimmy, pantomime, and trade partners.

A tall, skinny, dark-skinned man squats on the curb with his knees pointed up around his ears like a cricket. He laughs outrageously, then returns to the task at hand, squinting in concentration as he mixes orange soda with a clear liquor. People shuffle by, and he gives them a swig from the bottle or pours a little into their cup if they have one. A chubby young woman in pink spandex cutoffs tries tipping up the end of the bottle to get more into her cup, but he juts out his pointy elbows, shooing her away like a mad accountant.

People are laughing and screaming. Dancers strategically thrust their pelvises and asses as if they're sparring, daring one another to go lower to the ground, to move closer to the pulse of the music. The scene is riddled with hooting, cackling, and shouting, and we walk through unnoticed by the dancers, ignored by the mute stone wall surrounding the cemetery. The scent of jasmine and eucalyptus wafts from the granite crosses and iron plaques.

My relationship with Alejandro will end tonight. It will end as a cycle of the moon ends—timely, predictably, and completely bound to nature—the nature of Alejandro's wife, her angry menstrual cycle lashing out at the man who impregnated her, the man with whom she bore two children. Alejandro mentions that his wife is entering menopause, and as her bleeding ends, so do some of the wild tides that always ruled her impulses. Now she's subdued and recalcitrant, fixated on a few things: that she will not continue her post as a middle-school mathematics teacher and that she will remain married.

Although he married in the seventies, Alejandro chose his wife, just as he chose the revolution, in 1980. At that time, he remembers half the city leaving on the Mariel Boatlift. "Everyone realized at that moment that they could leave and start a new life in Miami," he had explained once in Bogotá, referring to himself as "everyone." Alejandro will never say whether he regrets not leaving, but he will eventually confess that he made a very deliberate decision to stay. He and his wife seem strangely and resolutely bound to this failing thing—their marriage—whose success, like that of the revolution, seems largely based on the fact that it has survived.

My relationship with Alejandro will end when this cycle has concluded. Like the winter solstice, tonight may be the longest night, but as natural, calculated, and unfailing as the solstice, it too will end. The inkiness of the night convinces me. I'm in Cuba, but even as night progresses, Cuba slips away. Every night Havana vanishes. Light, energy, and electricity drain from the city, and it disappears. Walking through this island with Alejandro, I realize that when light reappears, it will not be due to humans' good intentions or stubborn machinations; it will be because nature makes it so. This is the only thing that cycles around in our blood.

I take in this walk and devour the conclusions I'm drawing from the filtering sky. I look to Alejandro. I can't see him, but I feel his face turned toward mine expectantly. It would be so easy to stop walking and lead him to the cemetery wall. I could press his existence between my ribs and the names etched in stone, and finally pin down esoteric Alejandro, metaphysical Alejandro. It would be so easy to humiliate myself by begging.

We continue to walk, and after a long while we come to a stopping place: a park and a bench that Alejandro informs me is close to Niurka's parents' house. Our hands are still clasped tightly, and for the first time since I arrived in Cuba, I turn and look him in the eye. Sitting still amongst the shadows, I can make out his smooth face and brownish eyes, always alert, clear, and compassionate. There's some light and, yes, it comes from the moon.

Eventually, I fix my eyes on a barren spot of ground near the raised and gnarled roots of a banyan tree, a small space of bare earth on this swarming, verdant island. As my eyes adjust to the film of light the moon casts on the tree, I see its base is sprinkled with stones and rocks. I let go of Alejandro, stretch out my hand, and pick up a stone.

"I'm going to tell you this first in English then in Spanish," I say calmly, finishing the sentence in my head with "because I must begin to root you out in both languages." Alejandro nods hesitantly. Once he told me the women he's known—his mother, wife, and daughter—have been the most destructive and volatile at these quiet, subdued moments. I roll the rock slowly between my hands as if it were a piece of clay I could shape. A moth swirls around our heads, connecting us with a flutter of its dusty, brown wings. Alejandro smiles a bit at the coincidence, but I don't. Now that I've introduced my intention and methodology in such a grave voice, I feel I might crumble. The white film of moonlight and the splay of stones begin to blur as my eyes well up and I crumple over, sobbing at first softly, then uncontrollably. Alejandro doesn't put his arm around me but begins to cry himself. We sit side-by-side, crying. He makes a deep, choking sound. It's the first time I've ever heard a man's tears.

"You're a bastard. Bastard," I tell him. "You've destroyed me. I'm destroyed, wrecked," I tell him in English. The Spanish comes off more succinctly because I don't feel comfortable saying "bastard," just that I'm destroyed. Alejandro cries and says he's sorry, that everything he said he would do he said in good faith, and that he never meant for things to turn out as they have. Whatever he does, whatever he says, it will be right because he's right, the right one for me anyway. I'd known since I got off the plane, no before then, that I couldn't be with Alejandro in Cuba, and now I realize why. He still possesses my heart and emotions. Only one thing remains: "I can't be your mistress," I tell him.

"I know," he nods, "but let me spend time with you and help you do some of the things you wanted to accomplish here. Let me be your friend."

I see that he really could do that: be my friend, help me enjoy my trip, show me how to get in touch with my roots and explore Havana. For the first time, I'm aware of our age difference because I can't accept his offer of friendship. I'm enraged. What I fell in love with—Alejandro's brilliant and generous mind—turns out to be too generous. I can't reciprocate. I'm enraged at his version of praxis: the books that never lead to social reform; the proposed symposia, independent of the government, that are never realized. For all the resolution this moment offers, nothing matches the rage I feel in my blood and bones and even my teeth. I must take this part of my journey with Alejandro set at a far distance, and already I feel the stone turning in my hands, smooth and polished, the ocean's fist, receiving my minerals and rapidly rising waters.

Una Aventura

Alejandro has enlisted me to interpret at a meeting of his work group. When I arrive, I find him pacing the porch of the beautiful old home in Vedado that houses his workplace. On my walk there, I faced a steady stream of men leering, hissing, and calling after me, and they weren't using flattering epithets like criollita—they weren't even using names. They were making sounds: low moans; sharp, wincing yelps; and every variation on "pssst" one could imagine. One man even followed me, finally trailing off after several blocks.

This has been my first long walk alone during the day, and I arrive startled and intimidated. Bogotá is all about boundaries and separation. It's dangerous in the sense that one feels crime, poverty, and potential violence pressing in from all sides. As a consequence, people on the streets and sidewalks move briskly and keep to themselves. Cuba is all about being connected. Police lounge on every other corner. People have inhabited the same rooms in the same buildings and neighborhoods for decades. If you step off the familiar grid or try to enter a neighborhood inconspicuously, everyone notices. Someone is always watching, and "island friendliness" can feel threatening, even lecherous.

Seeing Alejandro's hopeful and slightly worried expression sparks my anger all over again. I tell him about my experience walking, and he starts to make a cultural comment about the Cuban character being one of flatterer and charmer, but I interrupt to say there's nothing flattering or charming about being treated like meat.

Aída, one of his female colleagues, steps onto the porch and greets me warmly. "I've heard so much about you," she exclaims. When I tell her about my walk and Alejandro's interpretation of what happened, she laughs in a rough, gravelly smoker's voice and admonishes him for being so stupid. I wonder how this intellectual, and most likely feminist, woman deals with the fact that she lives in a city where a woman can't walk alone without being incessantly harassed. I'm sure her advice would *not* be "make sure you never go anywhere alone," but I have no idea what it would be.

Alejandro's work group is mediating a meeting between different representatives of groups of small farmers. These groups are exploring ways of making agricultural collectives "viable."

"Alejandro, can we get some pens and paper over here?" a short, squat woman with tiny beads of sweat forming on her pale forehead shouts from the other side of the room in very rudimentary Spanish. Alejandro jumps to attention and asks one of the other group members to look for the supplies. He introduces me to Ms. Simon from an institute of agricultural studies based in New York. Despite her loud voice and brusque manner, her handshake is surprisingly limp, "Darling, thank you so for translating this conference. We really appreciate it," she says in an effusive voice, and before I can finish my disclaimer that I'm not a professional interpreter, she's shouting commands at her husband, an older man slumped in the corner, and her son, a ten- or eleven-year-old boy furiously punching buttons on a Nintendo.

Slowly, the farmers begin to file in. They are leaders of collectives in Nicaragua, Ecuador, Guatemala, and Mexico. Alejandro introduces me to each one. All are soft-spoken and gracious, with warm, firm hand-shakes. They make me think of my adopted uncle—the husband of my mother's best friend. Now many years deceased, he was a cattle rancher, a war veteran—stubborn and sometimes bigoted, but possessed of this same humility and strength. I feel at home among these men, but increasingly nervous about my role as interpreter as the participants take their seats in a U-shaped formation and I'm placed at the head of the table. Ms. Simon starts to speak, and I struggle to catch up with her. She uses terms such as *crop rotation* that I have no idea how to translate. I stumble, pause, find a few good paraphrases, and move on. The participants are patient. Alejandro is glowing with pride in the far corner of the room.

Ms. Simon rapidly taps a pen on the table as she waits for me to finish her sentences. She's sweating profusely and, after a few minutes, she holds up her hands in a T like a referee and says, "Can we take a break?" She turns to me and smiles curtly, "That's all we'll be needing from you, dear." Fernando, Alejandro's boss, approaches her, and they retreat into a corner. He's tall and lanky, wearing loose-fitting jeans and a T-shirt. Despite his disheveled appearance, Fernando is consider-ably high up on the academic-intellectual totem pole. He's bent over, listening considerately to Ms. Simon as she progressively raises her voice and taps on her watch with escalating insistence. I give Alejandro a sidelong glance. He shrugs and smiles optimistically, but finally goes over to help smooth out the situation.

At the lunch break, he confides that the group had to save, scrounge, barter, and beg to get every scrap of supplies and morsel of food for the conference. He runs off to help locate an official, professional interpreter, which will cost dollars, and I take a seat at the table with his colleagues, Aída and Lissette. I break the tension by saying, "That woman should be working on Wall Street, not representing farmers." They laugh, but add that they know Ms. Simon means well and her attitude isn't reflective of all Americans. They say this sincerely and warmly, as if they've thought it through and believe it. I think how stereotypical and true the moment is—the humble, salt-of-the-earth farmers, the long-suffering socialists, and the rude, domineering Americans. Occasionally, the stereotype presents itself as reality, just like now. How much of the travel experience becomes trying to untangle oneself from these moments? We spend the next hour talking about Ms. Simon, the farmers, Cuba, and the United States. Maybe I don't have the skills of a professional interpreter, but it occurs to me that I couldn't have had that conversation, or even a good laugh with these women, even three months ago. That means something to me. In the end, sweaty Ms. Simon, her henpecked husband, and bored son were the only ones in the room who needed an interpreter anyway.

Both of Alejandro's female colleagues treat me like a friend, and I am grateful for that. Later, when we have a few minutes alone during the coffee break, Aída confides that she's disappointed, even angry with Alejandro for the mess he's made of his marriage and our relationship. "I swear to you, Ale isn't the type for *aventuras*. He's a decent man, a very decent man," she says, stabbing her cigarette in the air to emphasize "decent." Lissette nods in agreement.

Alejandro had told me that both Aída and Lissette were taken aback when he confided in them about me, but when they saw he was serious about ending his marriage and clearly in love, they were slowly won over. I feel strange around these bright, compassionate intellectuals. Alejandro's presence is so palpable. How easily I could step into their fold and spend the next few weeks intellectually engaged and emotionally safe. I could be Alejandro's mistress. Yet as I watch his work group shuffle papers and huddle together to discuss the organization of the talk; as they write out name tags for the guests and pool together resources to give each participant a pen and some paper; as Alejandro looks at me with pride and admiration, and his colleagues periodically squeeze my arm and ask me if I need anything, I realize I already am his mistress. That's what I've been all along.

My mother is in my father's apartment with him. A woman approaches down the hall outside. The brisk clicking of her pencil-thin high heels announces her arrival with the urgency of a telegraph. After a brief pause, the woman knocks. When my mother opens her mouth to say something, my father puts his finger to his lips and whispers, "Sssh." The knocking is insistent. After several tries, the heels retreat, spiking the silence with their staccato complaint.

"Who was that?" my mother asks.

My father shrugs and replies smugly, "Just someone who wants to have 'an adventure' with me."

I've heard this anecdote many times. Over the years, my mother developed a repertoire of glib anecdotes about her pregnancy and my birth, in which my father made a few guest appearances as mysterious foreigner and all-around villain. We visited my grandmother every Christmas until I was eighteen, and on those road trips to and from Kentucky, trapped in the car together, she couldn't easily escape my questions. I would cringe and sit through this anecdote over and over—the apartment, the high heels, the insistent knocking—all the way to the unbearable punch line. I thought if I tolerated it and just listened, one time my mother would keep talking, and something better about my father might surface—at least more informative if not at all noble.

After a while, I came to resent my mother and her stories. I thought she had made it her mission to convince me of how horrible my father was. I always intuited the meaning of the euphemism *adventure*. Still, the English version sheltered me. What child of the seventies could hear "adventure" associated with her father and not envision a barrel-chested, well-meaning Clark Kent with a steely glint in his eye and a cape fluttering behind him?

Today for the first time I hear the word outside of the context of my mother's bravura punch line. I hear it in Spanish, exactly as it would have originated in my father's mind: una aventura, an affair, a fling, a fleeting sexual encounter. My father shushed my mother and made her sit in silence on the other side of the door from his next sexual conquest. He didn't defend himself, rationalize, or even lie in consideration of my mother's feelings. Stripping away the English, it's clear to me that my father wanted to let my mother know that she was not the only woman in his life, and he chose the cruelest way possible of doing so. Could my mother feel the thrust of this word in my father's watered-down English? If she could have understood the word in his native tongue, would she have stayed in that room? Later, I'll learn she had her own motives for staying with my father. My mother was trying to escape forces much more distressing than his machismo.

Alejandro walks me to the curb and gushes that I did a good job. "Well, I don't think the United Nations is going to be beating down my door any time soon," I joke. He has a razor burn along his left jawline. We're both squinting in the bright sunshine. He holds a folder over our heads, trying to manage enough shade for eye contact. I look down at the sidewalk.

"They really liked you, so I'm going to talk to the group about getting together for the tertulia," he smiles.

"OK. That would be nice." I try to return the smile.

Alejandro squints into the sun, attempting to make eye contact with me. I concentrate on the small hole along the seam of the pocket of his meticulously pressed cotton shirt. Where is his cape? Where is his steely gaze? I'm on the verge of disappearing. Part of me wants him to rescue me, but my immediate instinct is to distance myself from him, and no better labyrinth exists than this malfunctioning, salt-encrusted, dilapidated island city. Given the lack of transportation, electricity, and viable phones lines, we both know this could be the last time we see each other.

I smile and step in to hug him, hoping a conciliatory gesture will cut the goodbye short. His shoulder smells like boiled yucca, children reading, and bicycle metal—the essence of his daily life, alien to me. I want Alejandro to smell musky and opportunistic, to reek beneath a fermenting aftershave that masks the true identity of a hunting animal. I need him to silence me by saying something hurtful, but he doesn't.

I glimpse a taxi out of the corner of my eye, and Alejandro waves it over. He negotiates the fare and I get in. It's just a couple of miles to Niurka's, and I could use the walk, but I'm not up for the catcalling. The *taxista* drives at a leisurely pace, never shifting out of third gear, which he informs me happens to be an idiosyncrasy of the car's as well. We pass people sitting and standing on sidewalks, some crumbling, others long vanished. I'm in motion, but Havana feels like a series of still shots: a chubby toddler stares over a woman's brown shoulder; a man squats in front of a bicycle with several deflated tires looped around his neck; a trio of tall, leggy, preteen girls struts around a corner, their arms interlocked at the elbows, their bodies unafraid of what they're about to become.

I should leave Cuba. I should return to Miami, reconnect with my friends, get a job, start writing again. I know this, but I can't obey reason. There's something more for me to discover here. I can't go home yet.

Yoel

I walk through Vedado, a formerly upscale suburb of Havana whose mansions and posh homes were long ago divvied up by the revolution and converted into multiple-family units. The second- and third-story windows are flung open. Blue, pink, and yellow sleeves wave from the ornate wrought-iron terraces and chipped marble balconies. Like eager children struggling to catch a glimpse of a passing parade, white, peach, and beige collars bob up and down on clotheslines made from miscellaneous bits of string knotted together.

It's close to Christmas and I'm on my way to see Odalys. On my previous trip, Alejandro and I met her briefly one day when we were having a coffee in Old Havana. We struck up a conversation about dance, and she said she performed with Yoruba Andabo, an Afro-Cuban folklore group. Alejandro and I didn't have a chance to see the group perform, but Odalys and I wrote each other a few times after I returned to Bogotá, and I intuitively held her in my memory as someone it would be good to contact in Cuba.

I pass an old man guarding a jumble of metal handlebars and patched-up tires and enter the UNEAC, the writer's union, located in a spacious, well-maintained colonial home. The space is used for small concerts and cultural events. People are standing around drinking Havana Club rum and Tropicola, Cuba's version of Bacardi and Coke. I catch a glimpse of the dancers dressed as the Orishas Yemayá, Ochún, and Elegguá. They are waiting behind the house to make their entrance. From a distance, I see Odalys, short and muscular, her deep mahogany face radiant beneath a cobalt blue head wrap. She's dressed as Yemayá, mother of all living things and goddess of the ocean.

The musicians shuffle through the crowd and take their seats. A tall, lanky, bucktoothed man picks up the two wooden pieces of the *clave* and strikes them together. The music begins in five swift beats.

Out comes Elegguá, leaping about playfully, the spirit of a child one moment, a drunken, staggering, rancorous old man the next. The skirts swish by. Ochún, goddess of rivers, birth, and sexuality, sashays to one corner, throwing her chest out, giggling, and waving her fan flirtatiously. She's dressed in gold and yellow, her arms ringed with bangles. In the other corner, Yemayá sits self-contained and proud, her nostrils flaring, her head rearing back.

A man who was standing now sits, his muscular form squarely centered on the *cajón*, a wooden box that African slaves once used as crate and drum. An hourglass-shaped *batá* rests in his lap. At his side sits a *chekere*, a round wooden-bellied instrument wrapped in a net of seashells. The man is dark-skinned and big-boned; his full lips scowl and his eyes lift up at the corners. These eyes are almost closed, but he projects the air of one who sees everything as if through Venetian blinds. His back is painstakingly straight.

Without warning, he lets a hand fall on the taut skin of the batá, discharging a single note that ricochets through the crowd. He opens his mouth, but the song emerges from his thighs. He alternates between the two instruments, drumming first the batá, then leaning forward to pound on the cajón between his legs, and occasionally striking a cowbell pinned beneath his foot. The song falls somewhere between a chant and a benediction, the syllables intoning downward and ending upward on a sharp, clipped *a* or *i* sound. He belts out a cappella praise to Yemayá. Odalys stands and windmills her arms forcefully, creating waves of blue and white with her skirt and petticoats. She turns her face upward, and it reflects the waves, torrents, and moods of the ocean.

The black man with the Chinese eyes seems to look at no one: nightshade crawls up his back. His right nipple is a flower pressed into his chest, the deep purple shade of a violet's mouth. He appears to see nothing as sweat rolls down his cheeks, and if I hadn't seen the beginning of the song and the initial bead of sweat grow larger and larger until it could no longer contain its own weight and had to fall, I'd think they were tears.

I'm standing with the rest of the crowd, but my body reaches for its own space. I don't want to dance with anyone. I don't want anyone to teach me. I don't need to know what he's singing or to whom. Thoughts of Missouri and its storms surprise me. When I was young, the tree branches around our two-room duplex shook. Like this drum, they rattled between the thunder and the silence that storms generate. I stand under it now, the tree from my childhood now felled, carved, and fitted with animal skins. The thunderous percussion feels comforting and familiar. It feels like an affirmation that something good might still come from this trip.

I put my hands on my hips and move to the music. I've moved this way many times. Dancing alone, I've lifted the petticoats of my imagination and swaggered through deep-running water. I've danced my way across, navigating the river where it forms gullies and pools. Now I dance to give thanks for this music, this moment in Cuba, and my surprising connection to my first home. I raise my wrist in time with the singer's voice; I hold it high, and the arc of the song courses through my veins. I've dreamed of this moment while my mother rested her eyes in the living room, the game shows vaccinating us with their bells and whistles, the calling out of three-syllable answers and synonyms. And I'd be in the hallway, dancing, praying, understanding a magnificent God, and forgetting him.

The Orishas recede behind the singer's final chorus; they sashay toward the back of the house and disappear, quickly replaced by recorded salsa music.

People naturally slip in and around the spinning pinwheel of salsa. Two men interlock elbows and take turns twirling a spunky woman in cutoffs. The men wrap their arms around the woman quickly, like layers of scarves. They whirl her away from them and reel her back in. They spin and turn her. She holds out her hands to both men, and jiggles her hips and thighs without ever breaking her connection to them. Their thrilling spontaneity and improvisation remind me of the DJs and dancers at the underground bar I discovered my first night in Havana.

Odalys appears in street clothes and squeals my name, greeting me with great excitement and lots of hugs. She introduces me to David, her boyfriend, a Spaniard with long, ashen dreads. She introduces me to the other dancers and a few musicians, among them Yoel, the singer/percussionist with the Chinese eyes. A song by Cuba's famed Los Van Van comes on, and Odalys commands Yoel to dance with me. He holds out his hand politely, and we hit the floor. We dance playfully. He has a wide, friendly, gap-toothed smile and dimples. When I turn the wrong way, he gives an exaggerated shrug, smiles, and follows me, but there's something intense, even regal about him: his strong shoulders and upright posture, his slightly raised chin and pristine white clothes.

We dance to a few songs, and when I look around, the entire room is staring at us—the band members, dancers, and singers. All eyes are on us. Yoel shrugs and smiles, "Muchos ojos encima," he says, tapping an index finger below his eye. I take him literally because I see people are watching us, but over time, I'll come to understand that phrase as a curse, something that will inspire dread and paranoia. I'll fear that expression and the power a look of envy and ill will can wield. Over time, I'll become scared to look around. But for now, I'm in Cuba, and I'm dancing with Yoel, who seems to sweat tears and sing in cries, whose drums make a visceral sound thump in my thighs and stomach.

Scrawny British and large-boned northern European women hang adoringly onto young, muscular black men. Hippy, backpacking European guys twirl stunning mulatas in long, flowing dresses or tight spandex shorts. I see Yemayá keeping her eye out for me and Ochún charming everyone with her fickle, coquettish demeanor. I don't feel vulnerable because I don't perceive myself as a tourist. My father is from Havana, and I'm here one last time to experience what I can of this island.

I don't see myself as a complete outsider, and because of my Cuban-shaped body and Miami expressions, neither do my new friends. Not quite an outsider; definitely not an insider. More than anything, fatigue has given me the illusion of invincibility. The Alejandro ordeal has depleted me to such an extent, I feel I have nothing left to give and, therefore, nothing can be taken from me. I couldn't be more mistaken.

After the gig, Yoel stands off to the side, a quiet profile staring ahead, removed from the shouts and giggles of the group. I walk up to him and he smiles. I hadn't noticed it when we were dancing, but despite his statuesque frame, he's only an inch or two taller than me. I invite him to come with us for sandwiches and beer, and he accepts with a reserved smile.

We head to an outdoor café across the street from the Malecón, where couples line up at snack bars to share a beer or a sandwich. Men in *bicitaxis* pedal up and down the street, hauling locals and tourists around. At the café, I notice Yoel eats slowly. He chews deliberately and doesn't drink alcohol. Several Cubans exchange looks when he pulls out his own dollars to pay for his sandwich. People are screaming across the table. Dancers are jumping up and running around, sitting on one lap, then another. Everyone's drinking from other people's beers, laughing, and recounting songs they've heard. Odalys is excited and distracted, hopping from her boyfriend's lap to me, squealing, "I can't believe you're here!" Yoel rolls his eyes and smiles as if she's a pesky kid sister.

A chubby, light-skinned man in a white cap launches into a story about how half of the group got detained at last weekend's gig and had to spend the night in jail. A fight broke out, and the police arrested everyone including the musicians, some of whom are quite old.

I turn to Yoel, "Did you get taken away too?" He scoffs as if the idea were preposterous. "I don't involve myself in stupidities," he remarks.

"Oh Yoel, always so well behaved," Odalys hangs on his neck and teases.

"Well, wouldn't the police know the difference between drunks fighting and musicians playing?" I ask.

"Good question," Yoel raises his eyebrows in agreement. He lowers his voice, but his tone is firm. "What they *know*," he says using my word, "is this," and he holds out his forearm and rubs two fingers back and forth indicating the darkness of his skin.

With Alejandro, everything seemed possible—Cuba was about art, dialogue, collaborations, and projects—the uplifting part of the struggle, but I sense something else from Yoel. I sense another Cuba. Is it a musician's Cuba, a black man's Cuba, or simply Yoel's Cuba?

People begin to gather their belongings and speculate on the possibilities of transportation. I feel like walking. I have too much energy to sleep, and if I take a cab home, I'll get there too quickly. Yoel offers to escort me, and Odalys leaves me in his charge. She promises that we'll get together soon. She'll give me dance lessons and we'll go to museums, although she doesn't have a phone and isn't sure when she'll be able to borrow her cousin's bike (hers is in for repair) to make it over to Nuevo Vedado, where I'm staying. Yoel steps to the outside of the sidewalk, placing himself between me and the occasional passing car or taxi. He holds out his arm in a gentlemanly gesture, and we take off.

It's late when we arrive at Eddy and Linda's house. We sit on the front porch, Yoel one step higher than me. I lean back against his chest. There are no streetlights or houselights on, no air conditioners humming or cars honking in the distance; no rooftops or high-rises punctuating the skyline, no skyline for that matter. Just the leafy edges of the avocado tree that droops over the side of Eddy and Linda's house, and beyond that, a vast, pitch-black sky full of stars. I start to tell Yoel that I haven't seen a sky like this since Missouri, but then I realize I'd have to explain Missouri, and why there aren't stars like this in Miami. I don't want to interrupt the sky with so much babble.

"Hey, will you sing something?" I ask.

Yoel pauses and lets out a few words in Yoruban, not quite a song but not quite speech. "This is where the singers ask Ochún to stand up and move her hips," he explains. "That needs to happen for everything else to take place." I've never heard a human voice sing in the dark before. Listening like this, suffused with sound and darkness, must be the closest we can get to a memory of the womb. From inside her belly, we're suffused with our mother's voice and, even more directly, with the gurgle of her intestines, the pounding of her heart. I lean back against Yoel and turn my head just enough to hear a faint pounding.

Whatever can or will go wrong hasn't yet. It's just the Cuban with Chinese eyes and my ear pressed to his voice. It's just the delicate moment of two people meeting, when the newness of their presence makes an inky imprint on the night sky. The moon and stars are visible in abundance from this spot approximately 225 miles from Miami because the streetlights, houselights, and electricity on this block, at this hour, have been cut. While the conductors, wires, and generators rest, night is held together by the invisible wire of Yoel's voice. It hangs in the air in measures, carving a cadence into the silence. It lasts a while.

I don't know it, but all over the block, people are watching us. I can't see them, but the neighbors are watching the white girl from *allá*, Miami, sitting between the legs of *el negrón*. Between the ravenous eyes of the neighbors and the cool, wet leaves of the avocado tree, Yoel bites hard into the back of my neck. Up until that point, everything has felt retractable. I could have continued sitting in the dark with this man. We could have arranged a time to see each other again and he could have left, or I could have gone up to my room and resolved not to see the same people too frequently on this trip. He nudges me and nods toward the door, signaling that we should go inside. I follow.

We sit on the sixties-style divan whose orange vinyl cushions and thin, dark walnut armrests are propped up on the original wooden art deco pegs. Among all the knickknacks—the angular lampshades, the plastic doilies, the candy bowls made of blue-and-orange blown glass—I wrap my legs around him. A gaudy Japanese-style partition with a black plastic frame and yellowed rice-paper windows divides the large room into a TV room where Eddy watches his shows and a sitting room, where we are and where it seems no one has sat for decades.

Earlier today, Eddy and I watched an interview with Cuban experts on the Elián González situation. The experts kept referring to Operation Peter Pan, and when I asked what they were talking about,

Eddy scratched his belly and said, "Well, that was when the Catholic Church and the U.S. government first kidnapped our children."

"But the United States was rescuing those kids," I replied. Then, realizing the dramatically different versions of one detail in a long history, we both backed down.

I go upstairs, carefully feeling my way along the wall, take a condom from my suitcase, and tiptoe back to the sitting room. Yoel is silent and expectant. Everything about him is taut and motionless. His brown eyes moisten, and in the scarce light, his lips radiate a deep pink. I usually ignore this part of sex, even look away, but Yoel does nothing. He sits straight-backed, holding himself. He stares at and beyond me calmly, his eyes half-closed like a silent Buddha. I take the condom out of the plastic wrapper and unroll it with the care of a museum keeper protecting an ancient statue. I climb. I climb this man whose song entered me when the high-clipped consonants began to chip their way into my consciousness.

He holds my upper body tightly and presses the side of his face to my chest as if he's listening. I remember one of the men in the band, a tall skinny man who played the *trompeta china*, a round circular trumpet. He had tilted his head downward, listening attentively as he played, and tears had streamed in thin, straight lines down his cheeks. At first, I had thought he was sweating, but Odalys told me that, no, they were indeed tears. "He cries at every performance," she said nonchalantly. This excites me, the thought of the man crying into his Chinese trumpet.

Yoel grips my shoulders and rib cage so tightly my entire upper body is immobilized, which makes me more aware of the soft angle of my pelvis and the swollen vaginal walls throbbing and clinging to his sex. I let my arms rise and fall, wave and slither like Shiva, and have no fear of falling.

Yoel is regal in the shadows of this prerevolutionary home. Everything he needs he places firmly between his legs like a proclamation—his penis, his batá, his plate of food, and his woman. Later, I will translate this night as, "Everything felt right." Midnight, moonlight of teeth, Yoel biting into the back of my neck. Later, I'll say Yoel's bite pulled me from the speculative stars and impermanent galaxies of Alejandro's metaphysical universe to the permanence of the sensual moment, the here and now. Like an animal reclaimed by nature and dragged off, I'll recognize Yoel's possessive and violent bite. It will mark the rest of my trip.

Ochún

Odalys invites me to her aunt's house for a *fiesta de santo*, a party honoring the deity Elegguá. Out back, people are sitting in a circle and chatting. There's a small makeshift shed on the edge of the patio, and through the half-open door, I catch a glimpse of a small iron box sitting in the corner. Odalys' cousin shuffles back and forth carrying a plate with various pieces of cake and candies. She places the plate in the little iron box, mumbles a few things in Yoruban, and leaves. Odalys says the food is for the saints and that Elegguá, in particular, likes sweets and toys because he's ornery, *un niño travieso*, as I've already surmised. Aside from that, there's not much going on.

An honored guest at the fiesta is Odalys' cousin, a tall, broad-shouldered dancer who once performed with Cuba's famed Ballet Nacional Folklórico until he immigrated to Sweden, where he now lives with his wife and two children. Like many Cuban artists, he left Cuba to do a performance and stayed. His wife, a tall, blonde Swedish woman, speaks comfortable Spanish and keeps a close eye on her husband, bristling just a little when he runs off to greet guests and craning her neck to look for him when he's out of sight for too long.

Yoel is present, wearing pressed white jeans and a white button-down shirt. His head is freshly shaved and his multicolored Santería beads gleam beneath his collar. We greet each other with a polite, formal kiss on the cheek, and I run off to chat with Odalys and her friends. Yoel's perched nearby, silent and intense, barely making a pretense at social chatter. I'm not sure what he's doing here or what he expects from me.

Someone says there's a Los Van Van concert at an auditorium near the Plaza de la Revolución, and a group of us start to walk over there. Yoel steps up close to me, which makes me slightly uncomfortable. I don't know how he interprets what happened last night. I don't know what to think of it myself. One of the Swedish woman's cousins, who's here visiting with her, strolls up to me, asking where I'm from and if I've been to Cuba before. His name is Simon, and he says that he's been here a few times before and now twice more since his cousin married Juan Carlos, the dancer. Simon asks me to repeat my name, then he immediately launches into what he's wanted to tell me all along. "Be careful," he whispers in English, "Cubans only know one thing and they only want one thing." He looks around cautiously as if someone might understand him and adds, "They're greedy people." I laugh at him in disbelief.

"Let me guess. You got jilted by a beautiful mulata," I speculate playfully, hoping to lighten his intensity.

"No, no, no," he wags his finger in front of his own face. Out of my peripheral vision, I see Yoel staring straight ahead.

"The only thing they know how to do is fuck." Everyone knows that word. Several ears perk up, and Simon's cousin, who's walking up ahead with her husband, yells something back in Swedish that sounds like a reprimand. Simon ignores her and adds in a low voice, "That's all they know how to do, and they'll use it to get whatever they can from you—clothes, dinners, money, a way off the island." I can sense Yoel tensing, straining to understand, but he's hopelessly excluded from the conversation. Simon's disdain quickly dissolves in futility: "They all use each other," he exclaims. He unzips his leather fanny pack and takes out a cigarette. Several people ask for one, and he dispenses them while shooting me a look as if to say, "See what I mean?"

His glasses are steamed up from the humidity, and every few minutes he wipes them off and dabs at his forehead with a white cotton handkerchief of a style that until then I've only seen Cuban men carry. At the house, I'd noticed his eyes were dark blue, but now they look black and jittery as he pats the bridge of his nose and his brow. I can imagine him taking what he can get from Cubans as well—men, women, little girls, little boys. Who has Simon slept with here? Who has he run out on or underpaid?

I lean in close and whisper, "No offense, man, but don't project your pitiful little experience onto a whole population and call it wisdom." This is not something I'd normally say to a stranger. Normally, I'd say the politest thing that would get me out of the conversation quickly, but after many weeks without my native language, it's liberating to air my opinion in straightforward English, and I add, "Do you really know anything about the culture? Do you speak the language? Have you tried to have an actual conversation with anyone?"

Simon throws up his hands, exasperated. I'd thought he'd be offended, but instead he looks frustrated as if I haven't understood some crucial part of what he's said. He opens his mouth and starts to speak very deliberately, "What I meant was. . . ."

I turn to Yoel and ask if we're close to the Plaza de la Revolución. "It's just up ahead," he points, and sure enough, I can make out the shadows of El Che's beret and tousled bangs in the distance.

At the Plaza de la Revolución everyone tells me to keep quiet so that the ticket scalpers won't recognize me as a tourist and try to charge dollars. Someone buys the tickets in pesos, and we enter the packed auditorium, where the concert is in full swing. Young men weighed down by gold chains, medallions, and Santería beads clutch their female counterparts, squeezed into white, Lycra bodysuits. People climb on the enormous speakers, hang from the rafters, and swing toward the stage.

The music is so vital, so electric that I feel I can do these superhuman physical acts too. Yoel gives me a boost, and I join a young man and two girls on one of the mammoth speakers. I'm sweating, shaking, and screaming along with them. I can't believe I'm seeing Los Van Van, Cuba's legendary salsa group unofficially banned from Miami's airwaves. The group's history is rooted in the seventies and the Communist Party's push for a massive sugar harvest (which ultimately fell short of its goal), but their lyrics hardly seem political. They write about food, sex, and daily life.

I know what they, as Cuba's most visible contemporary music group, symbolize, so I'd expected them to be more activist. What I hear instead is, "Is that an overripe fruit or a woman walking by?" Their brand of bawdy humor and clever double entendres strike me as distinctively Cuban. How ironic that the largest group of Cubans outside the island cannot turn on the radio and hear Los Van Van's music, while stations in New York, Chicago, Los Angeles, and all over the United States give them ample airtime. As we file out of the auditorium, I wish I had someone to share my thoughts with, then realize suddenly that this is the kind of thing Alejandro and I would have spent hours analyzing. My stomach clenches with anxiety as a wave of sadness rolls over me.

Walking along the street, I count dozens of discarded condoms and *mani* wrappers, the white paper cones street vendors sell peanuts in. It's dark and after a few blocks, the group starts to disperse. Yoel is silent and steadfast at my side. Odalys calls out, telling him to look after me. I expect to see Simon shaking his head in dismay, but he's up ahead talking with a young man and woman from the concert. His arms rise and fall stiffly as he tries to express himself in Spanish. I pause then start to explain to Yoel why I haven't said much to him so far, that I'm not sure what he's expecting, and that I don't even know what I want. He looks at me sharply and asks, "Do you want me to walk you home or not?" Then he smiles broadly, and we take off.

We walk, and again, his voice resonates in the air. His song flows so naturally from his speaking voice, it sounds almost like an offhand comment or a thought that accidentally slips into the speaking world. I recognize nothing of the low-slung Yoruban vowels with their sharp upward swing, occasionally picking out only the names of Orishas in brilliant moments of clarity—Ochún, Changó, Yemayá—like lights strung through dark trees.

The occasional stench of rotten fruit rinds or layers of trash piled up on a corner is pungent in the humid air, but not repulsive. For once, the city doesn't disappear into the darkness of nightfall. Tonight, Havana is a creature sprawling; we stay close to the perimeter and feel our way around. The ocean makes the low groan of a sleeping animal, and above the raspy rise and fall of its throat and the random twitching of dreaming eyelids, Yoel sings. Truly, he sings.

We walk past wide-open lawns and promenades. Yoel points out the University of Havana, and I barely recognize the pillars and stairs where I sat with Alejandro. He tells me about his first trip to Mexico. Every night, he hid his earnings in his suitcase and then he just sat there with it, waiting to return home. He wouldn't even go down to eat for fear of losing his money. He tells me when he was twelve, he was reading a newspaper and some tourists took his picture. They wanted to chat with him, but he had to tell them no, because at the time it was illegal to talk to tourists. We walk and talk and the buildings start to sit closer and closer, until finally, they are a jumble of brick and stone, some structures preserving their European design, others crumbling. Yoel presses me firmly against a cracked, peeling wall and bites my neck and shoulders.

High ceilings. A fan from a radiator spinning on a wooden pole. *El cuarto rosado*—a state-owned room. Someone's watching. Someone's always watching.

Yoel leaves his identification with a fat man sitting behind a little window, and we enter one of the rooms rented to couples in fifteen-minute increments. El cuarto rosado, the pink room with the high ceiling.

Two long planks impose a splintery X across the tall French doors that once led to a balcony. This room was once privileged and elegant.

I can imagine its flower-laden veranda and a porcelain bidet. Someone once wore a white cotton shift in this room. Someone dipped a comb in violet water and pulled it through her hair in long, languid strokes, unburdened by time or responsibility.

Yoel sits between me and the room's grimy reincarnation. I balance my shins on the tops of his thighs, so that I touch nothing in the room but him. The dark air is stifling, and Yoel's chest is immediately slick with sweat. His breath floats into my face, neck, and chest in warm, sweet thrusts. The pink room holds me on the tip of its tongue. In the pink room, I stand at the edge of the world.

Our time is up. I have to go to the bathroom. Yoel nods in the direction of a streaked plastic shower curtain, and when I step to the other side, I see a commode—silent, full, and darkly laden with swamp-like algae and feces. We're out of time here, but I have hours to kill before he can return me to Nuevo Vedado because I don't want to wake Eddy and Linda. Yoel collects his ID, we exit, and I realize we're in the center of the city. Buildings and unlit streetlights stand around us. I can see only a few feet in front of me, but again I make out the white paper cones and used condoms—these things flattened under the ill-fitting shoes of Havana's citizens; their hunger and desire temporarily stamped out.

Yoel walks swiftly and purposefully. He leads me to the corner of Chacón and Tejadillo, where he's resided his entire life. We step into the large decaying structure of the apartment building. At its center are the remnants of a roomy plaza that must have been breathtaking at one time. We climb wide marble stairs, stepping over feces and debris. On every landing, an acrid smell hits me. Around the corner, a radio that's lost its station broadcasts a high-pitched squeal. We climb five or six flights; enter a narrow, enclosed staircase; and emerge on the roof of the building. A small dog chained to a wash table starts to dance and pee and whimper. Yoel lunges toward it and stamps his foot, startling me. The dog cowers, its scrappy little tail trembling with restrained joy. Yoel deigns to give it a pat on the head.

We enter a warm, windowless room divided into three sections by a T-shaped plywood structure. The front room has a couple of chairs, a TV, pans hanging in the corner, and a hot plate. We brush through a curtain and lie down on a hard board. Yoel's mother is sleeping on the other side of the plywood. I hear her kicking off her sheets and can almost feel her hoarse breathing on my neck. I doze off and wake up with a start. My kidneys ache.

Yoel is shuffling around in the front room, and I ask him for a bathroom. He points at the floor in the corner. It's so dark I can hardly see, but I distinctly remember noting upon entering the room that there was no bathroom. I give him a puzzled look, and he nudges me a little more toward the corner and closes a curtain around me. I look around and see a towel hanging on a nail, a metal bucket with some brushes and rags inside. Adjusting to the darkness, my eyes begin to distinguish one place in the corner that's slightly darker than the rest of the floor—a hole. I stand over the dark hole in the floor for a couple of minutes, open the curtain, and tell Yoel I'm ready to leave.

He walks me home. He has one arm around me and one arm guiding his bicycle. We walk in silence. A fog dissolves between our fingers as we cross town and emerge on the other side of morning. It's dark. The sun is still blue. Thin men and women wait on corners with plastic bags pressed to their hips. Lines start to form for coffee and guarapo.

Yoel talks about Ochún, the Afro-Cuban deity who's a counterpart to Cuba's patron saint, Nuestra Señora de la Caridad del Cobre. She's the deity of rivers, birth, and sexuality. He describes the gold piping of her dress and her twelve *doncellas*. "Why does she have twelve maidens attending her?" I ask. He considers my question as if amused and answers, "Because she gets in a lot of trouble when left to her own devices."

The sky is the color of tobacco leaves, then bourbon. It seems as if light will never come. The sun is dark gray, then slate, then blue, and finally husk colored. In Yoruban, Yoel sings the word *star*, then sings another word to emphasize the word *star*. He is the beginning of three songs: The first one I heard him play at the UNEAC. The second he sang to me on the porch at Eddy and Linda's. The third one is the song almost sung—the withheld, the promised.

Mireya

The following evening, Yoel asks me to meet him at La Lluvia de Oro, a popular hangout in Old Havana. It's a large open space with a long, sturdy, wooden bar to one side and wide windows latticed by iron grates on the other. From the entrance, I can see an all-female ensemble singing *son* and salsa at the far end. Couples and small groups are sipping from bottles of Cristal, the national beer. A large, squat woman sits on a rickety chair outside the bathroom holding a small chipped plate of coins and thin squares of toilet paper for sale.

When I walk in, Yoel is sitting at the bar nursing a soda. He spots me immediately, and his chest puffs out. He looks to the bartender as if to say, "See," and the skinny man wiping down the counter shrugs and responds with "no es fácil," the ubiquitous Cuban equivalent of "yeah, well." Everyone stares at us for a few seconds, then returns to their conversations. "Let's get out of here," Yoel announces loudly, and we take off. On the way out, I notice people on their way home from work who stop and stand with *jabas* (plastic shopping bags) dangling at their sides. They slouch with fatigue behind La Lluvia de Oro's dark iron lattice and listen to the music.

Once in the street, Yoel steps to the outside of the crumbling sidewalk and offers me his arm. After a few blocks, he gives me a warm kiss, then we keep walking. He tells me the bartender was about to throw him out, saying he was "loitering" even though he bought a Coke. Before I can respond or ask a question, he changes the subject. "You wanna run an errand with me?" he smiles mysteriously. He relaxes his arm and clasps my hand, lengthening his walk to long, purposeful strides.

"Okay," I respond, adjusting my bag so that I can walk faster. "Where to?" We've already made it to the fringes of Old Havana, where there are fewer people but still a steady trickle of workers on their way home and the omnipresent men and children hanging out in doorways and on front steps. Yoel takes my bag and pulls the strap over his shoulder, grinning at the thought of what he must look like sporting a colorful Colombian *mochila*. We stop on a corner and wait for a *colectivo* to pass by.

"I ran into someone today who gave me the address of a distant cousin who might know something about my old man," Yoel declares, looking straight ahead and then craning his neck to the right, trying to spot an old Chevy or Buick that might pick us up. Did I miss an entire conversation about his father, or is he expecting me to ask more? Before I can say anything, he adds, "My father disappeared during El Mariel. I haven't seen him since."

"Disappeared?" I ask. I know that more than a hundred thousand people left Cuba in 1980 in the Mariel Boatlift. Some criminals, political prisoners, and "undesirables" were forced to leave, but the majority left of their own accord.

"Well, you know, he left. Anyway, I haven't seen him since, and this cousin of his might have information."

"Okay, let's check it out," I say. A mammoth Chevy crammed with people pulls up to the curb. We squeeze in and ride in silence. Several stops later, we climb out and start walking. Yoel seems to know where he's going, but then he pulls out a scrap of brown paper—the kind grocery bags are made of—scrunches up his face, and turns to walk in the opposite direction. I follow. We're in Vedado. This much I know from the large trees and stately homes.

The main streets of Vedado run diagonally and end at the Malecón. On a map they look like slanted strings ending in the wooden base of a harpsichord. As we walk, glass crunches under my shoes or the street dips occasionally, and I lose my footing a little. It's getting dark. Finally, after what seems like hours of backtracking, crisscrossing, and knocking on a few random doors, we arrive.

Mireya lives in the converted garage of a large house that's been dismantled and reconstructed into a strange, lumbering construction of hanging plants, empty bottles, and numerous doors. Perhaps she inhabits part of the house too, but we never get beyond the garage room, which is strewn with stacks of old newspapers and limp cardboard boxes. Mireya greets Yoel with great Cuban fanfare. She hugs, kisses, raves, and exclaims how big/handsome/macho/*guapo* he is. After a few minutes of this, she pauses. "Now, whose son are you?"

"Eduardo's," he replies.

"Ah, sí," then more fanfare.

This exchange repeats itself a few more times with slight variations until finally she invites us to make ourselves at home. I take a seat and sink with a thud into the springless cushion of an old sofa. Pulling a bottle half-filled with a thick brown liquid from an unplugged refrigerator and handing it to me, Mireya chatters breathlessly about her life alone, her retirement from a local factory, and her aching bunion that may require surgery if she can persuade the cousin of an uncle in Miami to send her anesthesia.

Yoel takes a swig of his potion and listens politely. Each time he casually mentions his father, she cackles, "Oooh, muchacho. Your father was a wild one!" and we both stir in our seats, thinking it's clear she doesn't know Yoel's father's whereabouts, but if we listen closely, we might at least get a good story. But she quickly reverts to her internal monologue. After several more minutes of this, she suddenly snaps her head in my direction.

"Where'd you get this cute Yanqui?" she asks shrilly, as if she'd just noticed me. After an hour or so of listening to Mireya dragging out soggy family heirlooms and relating a number of tall tales featuring a hot-tempered man with a predilection for playing the numbers who *could* be Yoel's father, we realize this story could be about anyone's father or no one's father—a knee slapper without a leg to stand on, a little tongue-in-cheek of nothing.

There's no fan or ventilation in this strange garage room and Mireya is working up a sweat, her huge breasts sliding around in her pink housedress every time she laughs. Finally, Yoel blurts out the question, "Do you know anything about my father? Where is he? Is he okay?" I slip my foot out of my shoe and touch the floor—even the concrete is hot. Mireya interrupts her monologue and utters, "Ay, Dios mío! I don't know nothing about that man. I hardly knew him when we were kids. How am I gonna know about him now?"

Yoel is silent and solemn as we walk home. I'm debating whether to say something when he mumbles, "The last I heard, he's living in Chicago." He makes a point of pronouncing *Chicago* with the *sh* of English. "He has a new wife and kids there." And as if meeting this loony woman had confirmed this, he repeats, "Yeah. He's in Chicago with his new family."

In Spanish *padre* is "father," but the plural, *padres*, means "parents." Padre, los padres. I wonder why *father* is the root word for *parents*. Why is the one who disappears given such a distinction? How does a father start a "new" family? How does he leave his old one?

When Yoel was very young, his father had been unfaithful to his mother, and she threw him out. Over the years he'd frequently come around and tried to win her back, but she'd never have him. Still, he lived close by and visited Yoel and his sister frequently. Between one day and the next (or at least in Yoel's memory), he left on the Mariel Boatlift. *He's in Chicago with his new family.* Yoel's story always ends on that line—the rumor he's heard many times—as if he were rehearsing it, still trying to believe it. He was nine when his father left, and he started playing the drums the same year. He had signed up to take guitar lessons, but there was a shortage of guitars and a surplus of drums, so they put him in percussion classes.

"Who taught you to play?" I ask.

"No one," he scoffs. "I taught myself by practicing hours and hours."

I squeeze Yoel's hand in the dark. Somewhere in Chicago, his father is riding the L or buttoning up a child's jacket while I hold his son's hand. The son who cried for weeks after his father left is now an adult, wandering around Vedado in the dark with a stranger, hoping to discover something, anything about the man who left almost twenty years ago.

In Spanish, you don't "play" an instrument, you touch it—*tocar*. The tactile relationship is never lost in the verb, and few instruments involve more touch than the African batá. You pick it up, turn it on its side, and rest it in your lap. Not playing, but touching—hand skin to animal skin—is essential. Tomorrow, Yoel will start slowly, first rubbing a flat palm in a gentle circle against the surface. He'll play, and I'll sit somewhere close by listening to the message he's beating out on the father drum, the medium-sized batá (the mother drum is the largest, and the baby the smallest). I will listen as the rhythm picks up speed and force, and just when I think the batá's insistence will reach its crescendo and subside, the beats will rain down even more persistently.

Until tonight, Yoel's presence in my life has been a magnetic force— I've been drawn to his self-assuredness, but I've also thought I had the attraction in check. He's been eager, while I've tried to feign indifference, but from this night on, that will change. We continue walking. Broken glass and rocks crunch beneath our shoes. We walk in silence and occasionally he repeats, *He's in Chicago with his new family.* His voice sounds stupefied, like a lost child parroting the one valuable piece of information the adults taught him for survival.

While I'm not foolish enough to think I can orchestrate a meaningful reunion between Yoel and his father, I also know I can't be the one who turns my back on him. I've just witnessed his father's drunken second or third cousin laugh and flick a mocking hand in his face as if to say, "Who in the world cares about yet another Cuban who set out for *la yuma?*" I saw the embarrassment and disappointment flash across Yoel's face, followed by a terse "good evening" as he pulled me by the wrist out of Mireya's house. I know that cringe of embarrassment mingled with a sense of entitlement. But most of all, I recognize the feeling of dread that comes when one longs for answers but knows all questions will be met with rejection. The desire to ask and find out is more powerful than any degree of humiliation or disappointment. This evening I feel sorry for Yoel—it's true—but more than that, I feel bound to him.

Every call I'd tried to make to my father began with Zoraida's icy "Oigo?" followed by a long silence and a sharp click. I would swear never to try again, to simply leave it at that, but after a few months or perhaps a year or two, the compulsion to call would seep back into my consciousness, along with the hope that this time things would be different. Conversations with my mother about who my father was and why we had no contact with him always ended in a glib, defensive joke or a torrent of her tears. Either way, I was left feeling as if I'd done something wrong in asking. If I can't find the person who will answer my questions, at least in Yoel I've found someone who truly understands what it's like to want those answers.

None of this erases the gut feeling that nothing good can come from this union. In fact, every step with Yoel feels both disastrous and inevitable. My tentative agenda of cultural tourism—to interview some local poets or perhaps look for the house where my father's family might have lived—suddenly feels utterly shallow and meaningless. I'm worn out. I should go back to Miami and rest. I should accept that I didn't find what I wanted in Cuba. I sense that Yoel's possessiveness is barely in check. I know he's the kind of man who doesn't love. He consumes. He devours. He doesn't give, he takes. But I'm willing to endure any kind of hurt except abandonment, and despite all these reservations, I'm convinced that because we share a similar wound, we could never hurt each other.

We continue through the dark night, his hand an invisible weight in mine. Yoel gives a funny imitation of Mireya showing us her stamp collection, how she trilled her *r*'s and rolled her eyes as she waved around pages of worthless antiquities. We laugh. Despite his stern demeanor, Yoel has a flair for comedy and can imitate just about anyone to hilarious effect. We turn off the street, and finally see the lights of the shops and restaurants on La Rampa.

Yoel says he's hungry, and he takes me to the Paladar de los Amores. He orders *hígado a lo italiano*: liver sautéed with onions and tomatoes. They serve us *congrí* and cabbage salad from huge platters. Yoel has a voracious appetite, yet he doesn't hang over his plate or shovel his fork gluttonously to his mouth. He converses, working his knife and fork with the efficiency of a skilled violinist. He scrapes each glistening cube of liver and every last grain of rice from an enormous platter. I look around the room, and when I turn to say something to him, I notice his plate is spotless, and he still has the gleam of hunger in his eye.

Año Nuevo, 2000

A few days later, I move from Eddy and Linda's house to Niurka's vacant apartment in Vedado, which is much closer to the center of the city. Dulce, an elderly woman who took care of Niurka in the last few months before her breakdown, keeps an eye on the apartment and me. Painfully thin, with a sallow complexion and liver spots all over her hands, Dulce peels a pineapple with a machete, boils water, and washes my clothes in an aluminum pail. She brings me a dozen eggs in a thin, worn-looking *jabita* (plastic bag) without cracking one egg. Dulce tells me she spent the last few months trying to keep Niurka out of an institution, but in the end, her hospitalization was inevitable. "She was a danger to herself," she states flatly.

In her carefully pressed, flowered housedress and small, wooden crucifix dangling just below the collarbone, Dulce strikes me as a no-nonsense, devout Catholic. I now believe that Niurka truly is sick, but I still don't know what to make of the confused, jumbled letter she sent me a couple of months back, claiming that many years ago, she too was a writer (a fact she never mentioned when I stayed with her). She was repudiated and shunned by the writing community because her stories were *contrarrevolucionario*, critical of the revolution. The rest of the letter disintegrated into a list of names and scrawled-out ideas I couldn't read. An old Cuban friend in Miami once told me, "In Cuba, if you're writing's good, you end up in prison. If it's really good, you end up in the loony bin." Was this Niurka's fate or did her high-strung personality finally suffer a breakdown? Even if I could talk to her, would I be able to discern the truth?

After a few missed calls to Yoel's mother at her workplace, the H Upmann cigar factory, I finally get in touch with him and tell him where I'm staying. It's December 31, 1999. He appears freshly shaven and dressed in white. In a transparent jabita he carries a photograph, four plantains, a white candle, and some paper to float out an offering to Yemayá. The picture reveals a younger, leaner Yoel playing the batá at the age of eighteen. Even then, he possessed his regal bearing and intimidating scowl.

We dance on the balcony of Niurka's apartment to a couple of bootlegged tapes he made of Erykah Badu and MC Solar when he played in France. Yoel tells me how for three weeks he was "kept" in a Paris apartment with two other musicians and let out only to perform. "The refrigerator was crammed with hams, cheeses, and sausages, every kind of food you could imagine," he boasts. Yoel says his managers locked up their passports until it was time to return. "I came back fat and with not one iota of French," he laughs.

We wander through the neighborhood. I've unpacked my two favorite dresses from Miami—a dark purple shift of raw silk and a yellow cotton sundress—both too lightweight for Bogotá's cold, wet sun. I alternate these dresses with sandals and tennis shoes. My thick hair has grown even more porous and wild from the humidity, so I tie it up or weave it in a single braid. Today, I'm wearing the purple dress with sneakers. We stop at one of the dancers' grandmother's house. The old woman has a *paladar*, or informal restaurant, set up in her living room. She scrubs the table and starts loading it down with large glass bowls of chicharrón, chuletas, congrí, and cabbage salad with sliced tomatoes. We sit indoors on patio furniture, a dog asleep underneath each chair and *la abuelita* three sheets to the wind. We toast each other with some clear liquor.

When I walk down the street with Yoel, no one makes lewd comments. Some people even step out of our way. I'm embarrassed to say I feel relieved. Wandering toward the Malecón, we dance wherever we hear music. NG La Banda is blasting from a ground-floor apartment. Yoel places a firm hand on my waist and starts his fast-step. He spins me around, and we laugh. He winks at a little old lady who shuffles by and stops in her tracks to watch the white woman dance with Changó.

We walk to the Malecón and dance by the seawall. It's still light out. A few cars pass by. Several taxis honk at us. Here and there couples dot the wall, embracing and talking. Men stand alone, casting out their fishing lines. I remember dancing with Alejandro in the same spot and brace myself for a wave of anxiety. I'm getting used to it. Back at Niurka's, we make omelets and fried potatoes. We eat pineapple for dessert and listen to more Erykah Badu. I'll write these details, but nothing will add up.

New Year's Eve in the little room with the horizontal mirror. At midnight the air is still, and we hear a few guns fire in the distance. Yoel reaches up and turns on the radio in the window above our heads. The radio crackles, "Viva La Revolución! Viva la patria! Viva Fidel!" Yoel rolls his eyes and laughs at the announcement. I try to laugh it off too, but my voice has a tinny echo to it. A chill rolls slowly through my body and my stomach cramps. On or off the island, I've never heard Fidel Castro and his revolution so directly and fervently heralded. For the first time, I feel I'm in the Cuba of the history books—El Che and Fidel coming down from the sierra, releasing the white-winged *paloma* into a roaring crowd of poor people. I'm in the Cuba people fled, the Cuba where many suffer and hold fear close to their chests like playing cards; yet here I am, spending my money, strolling up and down the Malecón as if none of it mattered.

Yoel's presence looms enormous and inanimate behind me like an ancient, abandoned structure. I feel small and trivial, like a tourist fidgeting with my camera. After so many years of wanting a father, of wanting my father, I'd thought I would find a sense of peace or belonging if I could understand where he came from, but it's here in Cuba that I've lost him the most. Here, I've forgotten him, just as I've forgotten what I had originally hoped to achieve on this trip. I've forgotten my father in the hunger that takes over and displaces the rational, the planned-for, the expected. This is where I must be for now—in this tiny room with the forty-one-year-old announcement jumping out at me from a radio in the window.

I roll over on my side and pull Yoel's arm over my shoulder. His body quickly comes to life and sends a jolt of energy into mine. He cradles me and runs his hand over my hip. He burrows his face into the back of my neck and hums.

On New Year's Day we roam all over Vedado looking for fruit. The markets are closed, so as we stroll along, Yoel yells up at random windows: a chubby woman wearing pink foam rollers and a kerchief tied around her head smiles down at us; a wiry, yellow-skinned woman looks at us like we're crazy and shakes her head no; and a robust young man with a shaved head points us in the direction of another neighbor. No one has fruit to sell. We finally buy an apple from a street vendor for $3.75. We'd intended to include it in our offering to Yemayá, the goddess of the sea, but instead, we eat it. The ocean is one solid band of turquoise beneath the translucent white sky. Yoel bundles up the plantains in the wrinkled wrapping paper and tosses it into the sea. The bundle floats and bobs on the small waves, and a couple of men several yards away exclaim, "Aché Yemayá!" in praise of the mother ocean.

Odalys' interpretation of Yemayá the other day at the UNEAC was mesmerizing, not for her technical skill or "aesthetic line," the features one might normally use to judge dance, but in the authenticity of her emotion. She captured a deity capable of great wrath and great compassion. Her flaring nostrils and whirling skirts unveiled the torrents of the ocean; her forehead, slick with sweat, and her shiny blue head wrap reflected the sea's placid surface and cerulean depths.

In Missouri, my mother is on her couch by her TV, rubbing greasy menthol ointments into her joints. She's happy, or maybe sad. She drinks diet Coke with lemon and keeps the phone close by. We stand on the seawall and Yoel sings a song to her.

Double Negative

A few days later, early in the morning, there's a knock on the door and it's Alejandro, smiling earnestly. My heart starts to race. Yoel's just around the corner in the kitchen, and I ask him please to wait in the other room while I talk to Alejandro. "I'm not going anywhere," he says resolutely with his chest puffed out, his right hand flipping an egg. I can't believe this is happening and briefly note the irony that I feel as if I've been caught cheating on Alejandro. I poke my head out the door again and tell him, "This isn't a good time. Could you come back later?" He looks a bit disturbed, then quickly recovers his composure and agrees to stop by after work. The image of Alejandro trying to appear cordial with me is almost unbearable. I'm more resolved than ever not to see him anymore.

Yoel's gone home to do some errands for his mother when Alejandro returns. I make chamomile tea, and we sit on a long, green couch surrounded by Niurka's baubles and family photos. I glance at the dark, circular mahogany table where she served us a spectacular meal on my first trip. She really opened her home to us, and I realize now it was this small space that allowed us the time and privacy to fall in love.

Alejandro tells me that Dulce, whom he doesn't know, called him one day out of the blue and said Niurka was in great psychological distress and kept asking for him. She also divulged to him something she hadn't told me—a few days before Dulce called Alejandro, Niurka had crawled out on the balcony, and the neighbors had had to talk her out of jumping. Alejandro says he braced himself for the worst before he came over, but he wasn't prepared for what he saw. Niurka's wiry, bushy hair had been cut very short and she was painfully thin, the skin on her arms and neck hanging in folds. Purple and green varicose veins bulged from her calves. I couldn't imagine the gregarious, effusive Niurka without her fleshy frame. She loved to cook and invite people over. What could have happened to her in so little time?

I tell Alejandro about the letter she sent me and the things I've heard from Cuban intellectuals in Miami about Castro's treatment of artists and writers. He listens closely with a concerned look on his face, and finally, he says he knows nothing about Niurka ever dedicating herself to writing. He says from his perspective it certainly looked like she was having a nervous breakdown, and the cause was unclear. "As for the other," he says in a low, serious voice, "I'm not going to disagree with the possibility."

"That's a double negative," I chide him half-jokingly, half-seriously, wondering if *doble negativo* means the same thing in Spanish as in English. Evidently, it does. He raises his eyebrows intelligently and looks somewhat offended. I feel my anger flaring up, but this time I can pinpoint it better: Alejandro won't ever commit himself to a definitive opinion: the revolution sucks. Niurka's a loon. I want to save my marriage. I want to be with you.

"You can never be definitive, can you?" I accuse.

"What do you mean?"

"You know, feelings, opinions—*yours.*"

"I'm definitive about some things." His eyes moisten; his gaze softens.

"Oh, please. Don't try to throw out assertions of tenderness and expect it'll make everything all right."

"No. Believe me," Alejandro sighs with a hint of anger, "I'm not trying to make everything all right. Everything's not all right."

I press one of Niurka's brocade throw pillows against my chest and cross my arms over it.

"Do you know how hard it is to have you here and not be with you in the way I want?" he asks in a quiet voice. "In the way I'd planned?" His hands are interlocked, and he's leaning forward with his elbows resting on his knees. I can imagine him trying to talk tender, temperamental Alejandro Jr. out of a tantrum from this position.

"Don't try to get me to feel sympathy for you." I start, but I amend my statement. "Well, you know I feel sympathy for you, but don't try to get me to express it. I'm the one alone here. I gave up everything to be with you. You still have your family and your work."

"Once," Alejandro pauses, "I wrote to you that on any given night, we might be looking up at the same moon. . . ."

"Damn it!" I interrupt, "I don't want metaphors. I don't want any more moons or stars. Metaphors are abstractions with pictures on top. That's all they are. Don't talk to me in metaphors and think you're saying something real."

"As I was saying," Alejandro continues calmly, "We might look up at the sky on any given night, in very different parts of the world. . . ."

"Wait!" I explode, "you're telling me you embedded that small detail in your analogy so that later, knowing you're a coward and you probably wouldn't be able to go through with anything, you could just throw it out and say, 'Hey, look, I knew maybe this wouldn't work, but we gave it a try.'"

"No, no," Alejandro shushes me. "I'm not embedding anything. The moon was always there."

"Jesus," I roll my eyes. "Look, I don't know what you're trying to do, but whatever it is, whether the analogies are apt, whether the metaphors gleam with meaning, I don't care. Nothing matters right now. I can't see. I can't understand. I can't commiserate." Alejandro lets his head fall forward and massages his temples.

I expect he wants to start looking forlorn and tragic, and I refuse to let the conversation go that way. "Hey!" I say, sounding more sarcastic than I'd intended, "I think you want me to be sad with you. I think you want us to cry in each other's arms. Well, I can't because when you leave, I'm a stranger here. I'm not even sure why I'm here. In fact, I think you should leave."

He scoots cautiously to the far end of the couch, where I've unknowingly pinned myself during the course of the conversation. I look down at the pillow clutched to my chest.

"I can see you're not in a rational place right now. You're not yourself. I can see you're only trying to protect yourself," he says, nodding at the pillow in front of my chest. "With most people, I'd be worried, but not with you." I stare at the gold fringe on the gaudy pillow in my arms. I don't want to cry. This time, I don't want him to see me cry.

"I don't know what's going on exactly, and I'm not expecting you to confide in me," Alejandro continues, "but I want you to know I did love you, and I always will. Whatever happens, whatever you do, even if you make mistakes, I know they're only temporary. I have complete faith in you."

I don't know if he hears the slight gasp that escapes my lips. If he does, he doesn't show it. This is the last thing I'd imagined he would say. I'd expected him to reproach or judge me. With his temperament, I'd imagined he'd try to make me feel guilty. Alejandro leaves and I sit on the couch for a long time. The late-afternoon shadows from rustling trees and floating laundry begin their descent toward nightfall, but I don't move to flip a switch or light a candle. I want to sit still with

Alejandro's words. As soon as I stir, they will surely dissipate. I sit a few hours with what I always wanted from my father. Perhaps I even had it from him—or from others—but I never realized it.

It turns out unconditional love is not the panacea I'd imagined. It is not all-encompassing or never-ending. It's as fleeting as any other kind of love, and as surprising as heartbreak. The only difference is it gives everything and asks for nothing in return.

Onelio

I had expected Niurka to be released shortly, and that I'd rent from her like I did on my last trip, but Linda appeared one day with her benevolent smile and a worried tick in her right eye. She tells me Niurka's treatment has been continued. She doesn't know when she'll be released, and they need to make the apartment available for her son, who's coming from France in a few days. Yoel helps me move from Niurka's apartment to a rented room, which after a few days also must be vacated. Finally, I rent an apartment above Mirta's. Mirta, one of the singers in Yoel's group, lives one floor below, with her two little girls and her husband, Onelio, who is a shoemaker and a priest of the lesser-known Afro-Cuban religion called Palo.

I move mainly because I trust Mirta's daughters, whom I met at one of the group's performances. They are eight and nine years old, and I feel nothing bad can happen with them close by. The elder, Yamilet, tells me, "I like sweet and salty, but my favorite food is bitter: green apples, sour oranges." The younger, Raina, makes me a friendship bracelet from blades of grass. They often yell up from their balcony, asking me to color with them or go see their school. We send notes back and forth via a little basket tied to a string. Living close to these children gives me a sense of security. After one month, I've finally unpacked. From here I can smell the ocean. Every day, I wonder what this trip is for.

Onelio, the girls' stepfather, has wavy hair and a reddish tinge to his dark skin. He sits with one leg crossed over the other, a cigarette smoldering between his fingers, and an amused spark in his eye. He used to have a shoe-repair kiosk near the University of Havana. "One day Mirta came by and left a pair of shoes to repair," he smiles slyly. "She never came back."

At this Mirta jumps in laughing, "I did come back. It just took me a while."

"I was waiting for her," he adds.

She rolls her eyes and smiles. Yoel and I are sitting in their living room having coffee. In the same playful voice Onelio tells me, "In Cuba, things will happen to you that you could never imagine." He keeps talking like this until I realize he's not just making small talk or speculating. He's a seer. "You'll experience a violence that you have never experienced in your own country or in any other country—and you've lived in countries much more dangerous than this one." Mirta becomes respectfully quiet and so does Yoel, but I can tell he's tense.

Onelio goes on to tell me that my grandmother was very religious, very Catholic. "She protects you. She guides you," he points his cigarette in my direction. "Ever since you set foot on this island, she's been glued to you."

By way of explanation, Mirta interjects, "It's a whole other cosmology, my friend, different than Catholicism, different than Santería." Yoel shoots her a stern look and announces, "Let's get going." As we're walking out the door, Onelio says that he can't ask for anything in return, or I won't believe what he has to tell me. Yoel looks doubly annoyed.

Later, Yoel tells me not to trust Onelio, and he tries to explain why he doesn't like Palo, giving reasons that sound very similar to the reasons the Catholic Church doesn't approve of Santería. It's too much superstition. It can be used to do harm. He does acknowledge, though, that Onelio has strong powers of divination. I can't say I trust Onelio, but I believe what he's saying is true, and I want to hear more.

On another day, when I stop by for coffee, he explains the difference between Palo and Santería. The *santero* works through the orishas, African deities such as Elegguá and Ochún, who correspond with particular Catholic saints. He cleanses and protects. The *palero* works with the dead. Onelio is a medium between the dead and the living. He can ask things from them, but they too demand things in return—ceremonies, sacrifices, prayers.

It occurs to me that Cuba itself is like one of these spiritual deities. I thought I was just going to come here and "discover" my heritage or somehow feel connected to it, but this island doesn't merely give, it exacts a price for what you take from it. Not flowers or offerings of fruit, but flesh, memory, balance. I confide in Onelio that I feel vulnerable here.

"When in doubt, talk to God," he advises. "Take refuge in a church. No harm can come to you there."

I'm on a rooftop in Old Havana. Maiya, Yoel's mother, is sweeping the patio and smoking a cigar. Yoel's freshly washed clothes hang on the line to dry among her plants and herbs. I peek into the front room and see the tiny black-and-white Japanese TV set sitting on top of the mammoth Russian one that broke down years ago. This is where Yoel's mom watches her Brazilian soap operas. This is the terrace where Yoel grew up. The floor is made of brick, much like Yoel's mother—I think the floor is made of her too.

Maiya has been a cigar roller at H Upmann cigar factory for thirteen years. Every morning and evening, security guards go through her bag to make sure she hasn't stolen anything. She looks me in the eye as she tells me this, then stares ahead, a cigar hanging from her mouth. "I was born poor and I suppose I'm gonna die poor," she winks at me and takes a deep draw. In the corner, Yoel's taking down his clothes and appears not to be listening, but I see him bristle.

"I don't have anything, but other people still wish bad on me." Maiya tells me that if the women in the factory see someone with a new scarf or a shiny lighter, "They compliment you till you wish you had never heard the word *new*." "A compliment is not even a pretense at making nice," she adds. People hide things when there's no need to. After all, we live on top of each other here. We all know what each other's got. I come home and smell what the neighbors cook. At 9:00 p.m., we all turn on the same telenovela." It's true. Every night the same soap opera broadcasts through every window of the neighborhood. The entire block becomes one large speaker—blasting the infidelities, unethical business deals, and inconsolable lovers of the protagonists and villains in the Brazilian or Mexican soap opera du jour.

Maiya tells me that several years back, they raised a pig on the terrace, and when the time came to butcher it, Yoel had become so attached to it, he wouldn't eat it. "And I'm sure you know how much my son loves to eat," she winks at me and laughs fiercely. She swings pails of water over the plants, a cigar in her mouth and *casco*—a white, chalky talcum powder—dusted on her chest and back, "to keep away the bad spirits." The scrawny dog strains against the chain knotted around his neck.

This morning, Onelio told me my grandmother was part black and part white, una mulata. I'd always thought this confirmation would be a relief, but I feel nothing. My mother used to tell me that she saw a picture of my father's family once, "and some of them were pretty dark." My entire life black men and women have told me, "You can't be white." And finally, reports from the underworld corroborate a receding Africa on the shoreline of my genetic pool.

Since I don't comment, Onelio goes on to explain how the saints love stones. "When the Africans came from Congo to Cuba, they carried all their secrets in their stones." Perhaps I'm a stone. Perhaps I'm a cold, sweet fruit.

One afternoon, we head over to the Malecón and stand in front of the *Havana Princess*, a small, freshly painted, double-decker tour boat. It was set up by the government about three or four months before to take tourists around the bay. The boat appears uninhabited. We call out and, finally, a thin man appears dressed in white. He explains that he's the tour guide, and when we ask about the cost of the boat ride, he smiles wryly, takes a deep breath, and launches into a rehearsed monologue.

"Well, for sixteen U.S. dollars per person, you can have fish, vegetables, and a fruit cocktail. For thirty-two U.S. dollars per person, you can have shrimp cocktail, pork or chicken with rice, and your choice of one beer or one glass of wine. For ten U.S. dollars per person, you can have a beer or a glass of wine and take a twenty-minute tour around the bay. With that, he purses his lips and flings his arm in the direction of the harbor.

I think it might be fun to go on the boat. It might be worth splurging, but I look over to see Yoel scowling. At the end of this drawn-out explanation, the tour guide, barely able to conceal a facetious grin, adds as if in an afterthought, "Oh! It is required to present your marriage papers at the time of embarkation." Then he turns to me and in a confidential tone says, "As I'm sure you know, Cubans can only board the boat with foreigners if they are legally married to them." He enunciates "legally" with a sharp staccato accent on each syllable. Yoel scoffs and calls him an asshole.

To my surprise, as we walk away Yoel's anger dissipates and he even chuckles, saying he'd heard about some Cubans who held a butter knife to the back of the driver of one of these boats and made him take it to Miami. When I wonder out loud how anyone could derive so much pleasure from telling people they can't ride on a rickety old boat, Yoel's face darkens. He scoffs at me and barks, "Jealousy, girl! Envidia! Didn't you hear a word my mother told you?" I start to say that we're not rich, so what's there to be jealous of, but he raises his finger to my mouth and says, "Ssh!" The sound is sudden and harsh, like when you first press down on a pressure cooker.

I'm reeling from the fact that I've just been publicly shushed, but Yoel doesn't seem to notice. "Get a grip, woman," he hisses, looking around cautiously. "If you don't watch yourself, something bad is going to happen to us." With that, he becomes aware of his own anger, shakes it off as if it's a pesky layer of clothing on a hot day, and puts an arm around my shoulder protectively. He strokes my jawline, "What am I going to do with you, Loca? You're like a little girl."

When Alejandro had talked about the greed and jealousy that arises among friends, neighbors, and *compañeros* (comrades), his words were always shaded with revolutionary idealism: "People don't want others to have more because they believe in an equal society for everyone," he might have said. But in Yoel's world, envy is something poisonous and predatory. It's a matter of life or death.

In Miami, people speak of political versus economic refugees, giving the former more credibility and prestige. Nonsense. I still remember the anxiety in Alejandro's face as he watched the bag of food and supplies for his family roll down the conveyer belt in the Bogotá airport, and now I see Yoel turned away from having a simple lunch on a boat. Of all the freedoms, isn't one of the most basic rights the freedom to board a schmaltzy boat and pay to float around in circles while eating an overpriced, overcooked piece of sea bass and drinking a wine recycled from the previous night's half-finished glasses? I think it must be the day-to-day humiliations—the almost indiscernible offenses of waiting in interminable lines or being politely shooed away—that really break people. In the U.S. media, the narrative of repression and torture is seductive and thrilling. The narrative of not having, to which the U.S. embargo has contributed immeasurably, is endless, monotonous, unappealing. It rarely gets told.

I carry buckets of water back and forth to fill the bathtub, to flush the toilet. "If you want to go to the bathroom, it's up the stairs. It's around the corner. It's down the hall. It's behind that curtain. Don't forget to pull the chain, lift the plastic stopper, hold down the handle, throw in a bucket of water." A hole in the floor, a commode, a lidless tank, a bucket. It doesn't work. It's stopped up. It's overflowing. Women sit in plastic chairs guarding the bathrooms of Havana. They hold out small porcelain plates with coins and neatly folded squares of toilet paper for sale.

I've never had so many conversations about shit and toilets and where to get water and how to get water. Boiling water. Purification tablets. Liters of water. *Agua con gas. Agua mineral.* Water. It's essential, but after a while, I feel myself restless and resentful of the dutiful measure of it. I will not try to keep a balance. I will spill everything. I'll break it. Lily. Sunflower. Someone's watching. Someone's always watching. Hogshead. Bicycle. Today, I saw a man balancing both on his shoulders—the blood dripping, the wheel spinning as he walked down the street.

I alternate my purple dress with the yellow one, sandals or tennis shoes, hair in a bun or one single braid. I wear my yellow sundress as a robe, a coat, a gown, and pajamas. I'm drained by everyday life. Lethargic lines wrap around las tiendas de dólar (or *dolor* [suffering], as we joke), then there's the desperate pushing once you're inside.

I obsess about what we'll eat tomorrow. There's no food. When we get some, the whole building knows about it. His mother appears unexpectedly. His sister pays a surprise visit and tries to skim a little off the top for her two girls. Mirta and the girls knock on the door just as we're sitting down to eat. I wonder if my money is safe where I've hidden it.

I'll fashion an angel from a candlewick and a ceramic saucer. I'll whip up a cake from boiling water. I'll shape a pair of shoes from talcum powder. I'll tire of trying to save, count, and conserve money while Yoel stands silently behind me with his quiet intensity and insatiable appetite for meat. Wherever we find it, I buy it. I place meat in front of him recklessly: pork steaks, liver, chorizo, chicken, fish. I peer into his scalp in search of new meat. I plow into him. I give him my pens and razors. And he lets me. He sits calmly. He receives. He is given. Active and passive verbs become synonyms when it comes to providing for Yoel.

I take notes and vaguely remember that I once had plans to interview Cuban poets, attend readings and plays, and comb the museums. Instead Yoel and I spend hours walking from one place to the next. We look for food in the dollar stores and farmers' markets. We heat water for baths and boil water to drink. We wash clothes by hand. And in the meantime, his mother's hungry. His sister and her kids are hungry. And everyone knows (or thinks they know) that I'm the one with the wad of cash. I want to run from them, but I'm fascinated and paralyzed. We sleep. We wake up. We fall asleep again and get up and walk through the city, listening to people, watching them.

Yoel wears two watches—one with a calendar, the other with a stopwatch component. Neither tells time. Yoel practices every day. He beats out the same hypnotic rhythm for hours: *Ki-ha-ki-ha-ki-ha.* When he gives a class to a tourist, he shouts it while the student plays: *Ki-ha-ki-ha-ki-ha.* Straight spine, shoulders even, he beats out variations on the *mamá batá*, the largest drum in a family of three. He does this for hours. Sometimes people walking by on the sidewalk below shout up affirmations: *Alafia, Aché!* They yell out the name of their saint. Sometimes he winks at me and smiles without missing a beat. The skin of his palm is calloused. "Some of my lines have been erased," he comments offhandedly. Playing has changed the lines on his hand. It has changed his destiny. From here, I see the ocean. I wonder what this trip is for.

I'm not a writer here. I'm nothing. At best, I'm a listener, an observer: the reverberation of the batá, the sheen of fat on a glistening piece of pork steak, the dust on the windowsill of a collapsed building. I observe these things from behind a transparent curtain, as if I weren't here. I wanted to arrive and say, "I'm the daughter of José, who is the son of _____ and _____, whose parents resided in _____." But there is nothing to say about him here. He is as absent in Cuba as he would be anywhere else in the world, and so am I.

Yoel frequently scolds me. When we're on the street, he says I'm too curious. I look around too much. "What do you need to see? What are you looking for?" he complains. When I open my mouth to explain or argue, the finger goes up. The "sssh!" flies in my face. I look around and see an island full of raised index fingers, an island full of dictators. Waiting for ice cream, or waiting to cross the street, he swats men away like flies. He hisses and confronts where I see no need for confrontation. In Yoel's world, someone always wants to dance with me. Someone's about to grab my ass. Someone's waiting for the right moment to shower me with declarations of love. It's like these scenes are being acted out without my knowledge until they hit the dramatic climax and Yoel steps in, shaking a finger in someone's face, cursing and threatening someone else, grabbing me by the wrist and storming off.

Early one morning, he leaves to get his hair cut. The door to the apartment has an iron gate on the outside, as do many of the doors in Havana. When I go to the door to step outside, I realize Yoel locked it when he left, and I can't leave. At first I hang out on the balcony, calling down to Yamilet and Raina, playing hangman by raising and lowering the little basket on a string. I worry. I fry an egg. I search for an extra key. I notice that Yoel has the top two drawers for his things and I have only the lowest one, and wonder why. I kick a shoe across the room. If I find the key, I will leave a succinct, crushing goodbye letter and never return.

Finally, I call down to Mirta. I've been avoiding doing so, knowing that once I say something, I really will be locked in this apartment. Instead, Onelio shuffles out. Mirta's gone to the market. "Okay," I smile, feigning calm. "I'll catch up with her later." I tremble with rage. I curse myself.

A couple of hours later, I hear the lock to the gate open. Yoel races in, absorbed in his own crisis—he had to borrow a friend's bike to go to a different haircutting place because the one he usually frequents was closed—and the bike he borrowed was stolen. He recounts this while pacing furiously back and forth. He had to make a report to the police, and now his friend is without transportation. "What a mess," he grumbles. "Nothing works in this fucking country."

I sit on the edge of the bed calmly. What can I say to match the anger I feel? What will be irrevocable and what won't? In one clear moment, I look at Yoel pacing around in the midst of his crisis. In one clear moment, an even clearer voice calls up from the bottom of the well and says, "Get as far away from this man as possible" and I feel a flash of panic worse than when I was locked in here alone. Maybe it's not him; maybe it's the people around him, but in any case, I'm in too far. I'm going to get hurt. Yes, a voice of decision rises to the surface during yet another mini-crisis, one of several that erupts on any given day on an island where nothing works or runs smoothly.

I can't say I argue with the voice of clarity. I definitely don't ignore it. These moments are very rare in my life, in anyone's probably. I don't act on it either. Instead, I articulate it. I repeat to Yoel what the clear voice just declared to me, and surprisingly, he stops his rant and listens carefully.

He sits next to me and wraps his enormous hands around mine. He listens closely and in a slow, serious voice says, "This is what I've been trying to tell you all along, Girl. You've got to be more prudent. There're people out there that would hurt us, just 'cause they don't have anything better to do."

"So you think I should get as far away from you as possible?"

"Are you crazy?" Yoel's eyes widen with surprise. "Of course not! We're in this together. We didn't come this far to let them get the best of us!" he proclaims.

Odalys has a party for her saint, Elegguá. "I need some good things to happen this year, *hermana*. It's super important for me to start the New Year out right," she explained to me with a hug when I slipped her a twenty-dollar bill. A party for Elegguá must be a children's party. Odalys decorates with balloons and whistles. She has a large table filled with cake and candies. She dresses in a white cotton shift, and when the children have eaten the cake, they wipe their hands on her dress, spinning her around and around, laughing and squealing. This is the ritual of a party for Elegguá. Children are the guests of honor.

Later, I catch Odalys staring at Yoel and me, and in a quick moment while Yoel is setting up with the other musicians, she looks around cautiously, pulls me close, and whispers fiercely, "I didn't know you were going to get really involved with him. Be careful. I'd say that about any Cuban man," she adds, her tone of voice sounding more like a prediction than a warning. My heart sinks and a feeling of doom wells up in my chest. I want to talk to Odalys some more, but before I can respond, Yoel comes racing over: "What are you looking at, Girl? What do you need at this party that we don't have at home?"

La Yerbera

My stomach's been upset, and I want to buy some fresh mint to brew a tea. Yoel says he knows where we can find some. We roam around Old Havana, and he pokes his head in and out of doorways looking for *la yerbera*, an old woman who sells herbs. After walking a few blocks, backtracking, and taking a few wrong turns, we find her space, literally a hole in the wall next to a structure that has been freshly painted and reconstructed.

"Abuela!" Yoel shouts, and an old, caramel-skinned woman with light eyes and thick tortoiseshell-framed glasses shuffles toward us. New, green tendrils and hearty weeds push through the cracks in the broken bricks and crushed cinder blocks where part of the building once collapsed. Several pots, pans, and buckets filled with mint, basil, and other herbs stand in a neat row against the wall. Is this homelessness in Havana (which officially doesn't exist): gathering your wares and setting up house in an abandoned structure?

We kiss and hug her. Despite her spindly arms and legs, she manages to hoist up a cinder block for me to sit on before we can stop her. "I turned eighty-four two years ago," she tells us mischievously. She says her father was *isleño*, from Spain's Canary Islands, and her mother was Cuban. She grew up in the country. Her father would plant rice, beans, and vegetables annually, and they'd eat off that harvest the whole year. They also had three cows. Her mother would give the newest milk to the youngest of the twelve kids, and her father would time the butchering of one calf with the birth of another. "He didn't know how to read, but he was a very intelligent man," she mumbles while yanking out weeds from the crack in the brick by her foot. We sit and listen for a long time.

While she rolls up bunches of mint and basil in an old copy of *Granma*, the Communist Party newspaper, la yerbera talks. Her voice is even in tempo and monotonous, as if she's reciting a history lesson or anthem: "I'm alone now. My brothers and sisters have died off. A woman poisoned my son. He's dead. My daughter's got her own family to worry about." As if she can read my thoughts, la yerbera looks me in the eye: "I decided I wanted to live alone and die alone. I'm not bitter—sad, yes, a little, but not bitter." I nod in understanding. Choosing to be alone, as opposed to neglected by the state or family members, might be the ultimate form of dignity.

She touches Yoel's arm several times as we're leaving. "Even though I look white," she says, "I'm really black like you."

"A lot of people say that," he'll later tell me.

I've had a dull, persistent stomachache for a few days, but one night, a fever slips into my dark purple dress and I stumble into bed, asking Yoel to close the windows and the doors that lead to the balcony. I ask him to close everything and turn the small window unit in our room on high. My stomach starts to cramp. My insides lurch and heave like an old car being violently jump-started. My fluid levels rise. My blood volume quadruples. I'm reeling and vomiting. Havana's flowing from my every opening.

After several hours, I fall asleep and dream vividly of the very dress I'm wearing, the purple dress that's accompanied me for so much of this journey. The dark raw silk swells with salt, water, fire, and perspiration. It whirls with dizziness; the wind carries it to the treetops and drops it carelessly. I dream of executions, and the dress stretches and expands like a fibrous membrane. It holds bullets, splintered shins, crushed anklebones, calcified corneas. The dress sweeps through the Plaza de Catedral turning over the palms of elderly men and women who sit surreptitiously on the curbs, revealing the soap and toothpaste they sell for coins on the sly. The dress flies through Havana like a dark wing, like a flag with an emblem I can't make out.

Two and a half days. Fifty-six hours of vomiting and diarrhea. I'm sick of this country and its fines: $200 for selling homemade candies; $350 for selling a box of cigars; $450 for enriqueciendo, or making too much profit. Onelio wants to set up his own shoe stand, but the license, permission, and fees cost more than he could make in a year repairing shoes. I want to vomit Central Havana into Fidel Castro's lap. Everything's leaving me. Nothing can enter.

The iron gate opens, the dead bolt turns, and shopping bags rustle as they are set on the counter. Yoel was going to buy me some chicken soup at a restaurant we went to last week. It's been shut down for enriqueciendo he announces from the other room. It's a crime to make too much money; it's a crime to do well. Clocks tell different times or they don't work at all. I tear sheets from my calendar for toilet paper. The days don't matter anyway. This city wants to eat me, fold me in its blue shadows, and devour me. Mani wrappers and used condoms litter the streets. Balconies lean into the alleys. Rats scamper into the shadows. This city would eat me, would spill out around me like a blanket and envelop me. I twist and sweat, throw off the covers, then bury myself beneath them.

Yoel has the windows open to let in some fresh air, and from down the hall I hear someone's radio emitting a gravelly, 4:00 p.m. address from Fidel Castro: "The children of Havana want to know when they're going to have cartoons again." His voice lurches, stops, then pitches forward. He's referring to the fact that as of late, the TV runs only footage of Elián. I've heard Yamilet and Raina complain about this. "The children will have their cartoons," his voice is now gathering its notorious momentum, "as soon as the Imperialistas and the Miami mafia return Cuba's son to Cuba where he belongs!" There's a pause where I suppose the crowd would roar if this were a public speech, but instead there's a brief, strange silence before Castro picks up again and moves on with his rant.

It's a spectacular day, and a fresh breeze flutters the curtain on the balcony door. I want so badly to be refreshed by the breeze, to eat, get dressed, and go somewhere, but I can't move. The best I can hope for is a paralyzed moment between one wave of nausea and the next round of cramps. I'm beginning to wonder how I'll get out of here or who will come help me if I don't get better.

Yoel comes bounding in the room and excitedly flips on the small TV set on the dresser at the foot of the bed. I cover my head with pillows. I can't stand TV noise under good conditions, and since I've been sick I've insisted that the TV be turned off. "No, no look," he says, rubbing my thigh as if to warm me up, "you'll be interested in this for one of your books or something." I prop myself up on one elbow and watch as thousands of children pour onto the Malecón and march, chanting for Elián's return.

It's a send-off for Elián's grandparents, who have been given permission to go to the United States to see him. A television broadcaster stands among the throngs of children, announcing that the government hopes to send Elián's school desk to Miami with the grandparents to keep him company until he can come home.

Shots from Miami show Elián loaded down with Disney and Power Rangers paraphernalia.

"He has everything he could ever dream of here," Great-uncle Lázaro and his daughter, Marisleysis, insist.

The scene switches to a panel of Cuban experts who analyze the footage of Elián and formulate the theory that he's being coerced by his Miami relatives. One sociologist points out the way Elián's head is tilted to the left as he stands in the doorway of the Little Havana home, waving to reporters. "This body language reveals a child in an incredible amount of distress," the man explains.

Yoel sits and watches the coverage attentively, smiling at the spectacle of it all. I know he has no deep convictions about the issue. Like most people I've asked in private, he says he thinks a child belongs with his parent, but also adds playfully, "But who could blame him for staying?" I put the pillow back over my head and ask Yoel to turn off the TV. No matter who "wins" him, Elián seems doomed.

Between the waves of dizziness and nausea, I vow that if I get better, I'll not let Yamilet and Raina leave my side. Where they clamor, where their little knees plant into the earth, nothing bad can enter. They are the only positive forces close by. As I start to drift off, Yoel's breaking and crumbling two pieces of casco between his huge calloused hands. He snakes his hand beneath my cotton nightshirt and brusquely rubs the white, chalky powder into my chest and pubic bone. He takes a swig of aguardiente and spits the clear liquor on the bottoms of my feet—*so nothing bad can enter.*

I dream about when I could move around and walk. I went strolling down the Malecón. Fishermen threw light bread at me. "Sirena, Sirena," they called after me, "Mermaid." Cuba wants to eat me, wants to shine my bones.

After three more days of vomiting and diarrhea, Mirta takes my limp wrist into her hand, peers into my wandering right eye, and says to Yoel, "This is something else." He nods in agreement and, suddenly, I'm up walking through Central Havana in my yellow sundress-turned-bathrobe, leaning against Mirta's body for support. She's a very large women unencumbered by her weight. Her movements are lightning quick, and she whisks me down the street like an electric tram.

We stop in front of a beautifully carved wooden door. Mirta knocks and remarks to herself, "The nightly soap's on. I hope they'll let us in." I feel my legs wanting to buckle beneath me. I have to sit down. I have to curl into a little ball. An elderly woman with light café con leche skin and high, elegant cheekbones answers, and Mirta, full of apologies, asks to see "the old man." The woman looks from Mirta to me and back again, then she looks me up and down and lets us in.

I see a very old man shuffling back and forth in the back room. He is a twin of his wife: thin, elegant, with light skin. One blue eye is blindly afloat in a milky cataract. His brown pants bunch up over a large, black shoe whose heel is a good six inches thicker than a normal shoe. He drags along his stiff left leg and the heavy corrective shoe unconsciously, his face absorbed in the task at hand, as he takes small glasses of water and moves a chair in front of a small table.

He calls us back and seats me in the chair. Several old photos, lit candle stubs, and glasses of water are placed on the table turned into an altar. Crosses float in some of the glasses. Others have small bouquets of white flowers. He prays. I recognize the Ave María and the Our Father. I recognize Jesus' name. Other prayers I don't recognize, but they are recited to the same cadence. My right leg starts to tremble and I hold on to the chair. I try to focus on the candles and glasses of water. The smell of basil and mint is soothing.

The old man flicks cool water and sprigs of *albaca*, or basil, on the back of my neck, shoulders, and chest. In my mind's eye, I see three people—the leader of Yoel's band and his wife with her fake weave. I see a girl who is always hanging out at their performances. The final image I see is a shadow, a dark wing. I feel upset and anxious. I want to cry. I miss my mother. In the midst of these emotions, I recognize that I'm not nauseated or dizzy, but I'm not sure if I'm really feeling better or if the intensity of the experience has just temporarily displaced the symptoms. The dizziness starts to slow down and the weakness drains from my body.

I move away from the altar and sit close to Mirta, who holds my hand and thanks the old man. He smiles gently and touches my hand. "They got you good, mi hijita," he smiles. Mirta smiles too and lets out a sigh of relief in agreement, but then he looks more solemn and declares in a matter-of-fact voice: "The people who did this to you will ask about you in a place where you don't appear." By the time we walk back to our building, I am just lightheaded. I can already feel my strength coming back, and for the first time in several days, I'm hungry.

The next day, we return lugging a large sack of plantains and *malanga*. The man wouldn't accept money, but his wife had told us this was the main staple of her husband's diet. I marvel at how close the place is to our apartment and at how much shabbier it looks in daylight:

that door that felt so solid and imperial just the night before is now rough-hewn and unpainted.

We step past a row of men sitting in front of the old man's house. They barely acknowledge us with slight nods and continue looking ahead, rolling their cigarettes, sipping thimbles of strong coffee. Mirta tells me they keep watch over the old man, who's known as an *espiritista*, or spiritualist. Because of his powers he needs protection. There are men like these on any road of dust and dirt or crumbled brick. They squat with their elbows resting on the tops of their knees. They perch in front of certain houses like dark owls—alert, invisible, seemingly useless. Some sit on boxes, some on low benches, others in rickety chairs. Some sit on the ground—men of various shades of earth, sitting and watching.

Like a doctor dispensing a prescription, the old man hands me a mimeograph with a prayer printed on it. He says: "Sometimes your dreams scare you. You wake up and don't remember them. Sleep with a glass of water by the bed.

"Put a bunch of white flowers out for your grandmother. Sometimes you feel a rush or a sudden change in temperature. That's her. She passed a long time ago, but she's very attached to you. She's always at your side, advising you, guiding you.

"Don't run around recklessly. Don't open the door suddenly. Don't answer on the first knock. Wait for the second one. Cross yourself. Wait. Open." He rattles off these instructions, embraces me, pats Mirta on the shoulder, and sends us on our way.

"What happened to me?" I ask Mirta on our way home.

"Mal de ojo. Someone put the evil eye on you," she responds with conviction.

"Who?"

"Oh, chica, you name it. Who wouldn't want to?"

"But why?"

"Bueno. First off: tremenda criollita," she teases, lowering her voice a few octaves to the range of a cocky Cuban male. "You live in la yuma, so they assume you're rich. It's happened to me for much less than that," she smiles, squeezing my shoulder. "In fact, the more I think about it, the mal de ojo was probably aimed at Yoel, but he's built up a resistance to that kind of thing."

I don't tell anyone about what I saw in the altar, but I quit going to the club where the group plays every Friday night, and after a week or two, I ask Yoel if anyone's asked about me. He replies. "Yes, Giovanni, his wife, and that dorky girl Julieta who you say is always giving you dirty looks. That's it."

Raft

I stay in the room.

Over the next few days, while I'm regaining my strength, and for the next couple of weeks before returning to Miami, I stay tethered to the bed in the little apartment in Central Havana. I read, take naps, write notes. Sometimes I touch myself to assert my claim on this anonymous space. Sometimes I say, "Yes," or "Wait"—to no one, to anyone. I stand in the center of the bed with my legs shoulder-width apart. I sit with my knees pressed into my chest and make dozens of tiny braids as if I were knitting. I linger on the edges. I float and let my hand fall off the side of the bed.

On the other side of my wrist, the walls shout and murmur. Teresita heard that Pepe and his wife got the money for their new TV from an uncle in Miami who struck it rich selling miniature flags. *Imagínate*, selling flags for money. . . . Lola receives packages from Italy almost every other week. . . . *Ya tú sabes.* Someone has rum. Someone has pork. A packet of medicine and school supplies arrives from Hialeah. New shoes and pink Lycra are sent from Little Havana. My neighbor's breath draws closer. I smell what she's cooking. I hear how well he slept last night. I hear the playful slaps and the angry ones.

The citizens of Havana have been listening to each other copulate for decades now. It's become just another small appliance sound, like the static from a Soviet TV or a cheap radio. But here, within the bed's four corners, suspended six and a half inches above the floor, we're removed just a little. Here, we nibble on cookies and sip pear and mango juice from small boxes. Yoel steadies my notebook as I try to write. It's the first impulse I've had to write since I started this journey.

Quietly, Yoel becomes the man between Chacón and Tejadillo. That's where he resided when I met him, and that's where he'll return when I leave—to the rooftop of a six-story building constructed in the

1940s, the top heap of the heap, the hole in the floor where all the shit begins and runs down to the bottom. He hasn't commented on my self-imposed seclusion or the fact that I no longer call him by name. Now that I never leave the apartment, he's become *tú*, and because in Spanish the verb so conveniently pockets the pronoun, he's not even that. He's simply a verb, an informal action that in its regular form usually ends in *s*.

Our days are filled with dressing and undressing. Our days are long with making lists and filling them. Soon, my flight will take off from Bogotá to Miami and it will be like Cuba never existed—an invisible stamp, an infrared flash on my passport. These last few weeks, I often give Yoel lists like the following: water—not carbonated; ham—thinly sliced (but if it's that ham that has the texture of bologna, don't buy it); cubes for broth; candles; aguardiente; and if you can find it, that thick, sweet, brown bread they call *pancake*. He leaves to fill my lists. He leaves three, four, sometimes five times a day.

Suspended six and a half inches above the grimy linoleum, which is glued down over the prerevolutionary Spanish tiles, we whisper, shout insults, egg each other on, bark commands, and laugh. I turn my ankle. He shifts his weight. I situate myself above him. I impose myself on the small mattress. We make moves, assume positions. But our minds are working harder than our bodies could imagine. Well-tuned homing devices, we sidestep each other's mental space, stomp through the brain chatter, and sink in deep, like climbing into dark boots or lowering ourselves into a canyon. We go for a long time toward that quiet place, that place of sound dislodged from the speaker's mouth. Here, we don't implore, beseech, lament, praise, adulate, or give thanks. Here, I'm neither neighbor nor *vecina*, citizen nor *ciudadana*, comrade nor *compañera*. This is a moment where the radio speaks through its loud gravelly beard and I do not hear it. I'm pre-radio. Nothing that manufactures sound exists—not the megaphone, loudspeaker, radio, nor Soviet television next door. Yoel hums just a little, a low sound from deep in his belly. I follow. This is the one sound the neighbors can't hear, not musical but tonal, below the radar, beyond the signal and the receiver.

Much has been said about *los balseros* and the rafts they build to cross the Florida Straits, but little has been said about the rafts that keep the island afloat—thousands of beds, mattresses, and cots of various sizes and conditions. Yoel and I board one. We press into each other's skin. We slip inside. Tucked away within each other, we find the privacy and dignity of an unguarded moment. Blue heat, our shoulder blades working up and down. Our torsos bending. Our wide, glistening foreheads rocking back and forth, reflecting each other. In this motion, we're saved, just a little.

Much has been said about those who brave the Florida Straits. Nothing's been said about those who man the rafts of Havana. I remember the skin on the Swedish guy's face—slick and clammy like some displaced arctic animal—as he pontificated on the malformed Cuban species and its predilection for sexual licentiousness. He told his truth so maliciously it became a lie. Food, privacy, freedom of expression: What if sex is not desperation but a form of resistance? What if the body is not an instrument for sex but a monument to solitude, liberty, creativity? What if dance is not precoital but mythical? In this room, we enter each other and take refuge. I will not step my foot off this raft, I will not ripple the placid surface with my toe until I've arrived.

On the other side of the wall, four and a half inches from his back and my outstretched arms, the neighbors examine a wrapper just thrown away. They sniff the air:

"So-and-so had coffee today and someone else has milk from the dollar store."

"Someone must have sent money from Miami."

"No, that one has a sister in Europe."

"How many eggshells did so-and-so just throw out? I haven't seen an egg in three weeks."

"Well, she can keep her fancy omelets and her no-good husband. If she only knew what he does when she's out. . . ."

Yoel pushes. I stand between him and the wall of the rented room. I can tell this wall was once as bright and radiant as the golden ruffle of a marigold. Now it's faded to a melted-butter yellow—even the walls become a wish for food over time. Each time he pushes, I pull him closer. On this raft, like any, we ask for the impossible. The very structure of a raft implies disproportionate odds. Flimsy pieces of driftwood, patched-up inner tubes, scraps of old tires, and threadbare pieces of canvas tied together and tossed to the sea. The essence of a raft demands a miracle. Slowly, slowly now, he's moving closer. Yoel rows between my hand and the leaves. He pushes, I pull, and in this gesture, we ask that the ocean be something that we would not drown in. We ask for a miracle and it will be ours—in part at least.

No matter what happens in the room; no matter what happens on this raft; no matter where the undertow picks up strength and pulls us under—at the temple, behind the knees, between the thumb and forefinger—later Yoel is at the door, pristine in his pressed jeans and cap, heading off on an errand. He stands in front of the full-length mirror, brushing off imaginary lint, straightening his collar and cap. From the raft, I watch him go. There's something I haven't told anyone, something even Onelio the seer doesn't know: My father's dead. I don't know the details, but he's gone. I'm sure of it.

At first, Yoel doesn't articulate it and neither do I, but a promise has grown between us—the obvious one: that I'll get him out. Everything else—the fact that I love someone else or that his possessiveness has driven a wedge between us—is just fodder for the evening soap opera. The real deal is this: he's let me in. He's let me see where he eats, sleeps, and takes a shit. He's walked me through his Havana. I have watched him look for his father and walk away humiliated, the non-light of a Vedado blackout erasing his proud face and pushing his heavy hand into mine. The only way I can reciprocate is to help him escape. We don't discuss the practicality, but we both know that once I'm back in Miami, I can apply for a fiancée visa, and whether we want to go through with marriage or not, because of the "wet-foot-dry-foot" policy, once he's in Miami, he can apply for political asylum and have his residency within six months. The immigration laws are different for Cubans. They have only to step on U.S. soil to request and be granted political asylum.

During my last few days in Cuba, we begin to imagine ourselves in a room similar to this one, but in Miami.

I recite a list of my paltry worldly possessions in Miami: a battered green Honda Civic, a thin Japanese futon mattress, a boom box from college, and countless plastic crates of CDs and books.

"Seriously, can't you see yourself in Miami surrounded by all of those riches?" I joke.

Yoel laughs, but his face grows serious, "I can see myself with you. . . ."

"I'll write. You'll play music," I mumble, letting his arms engulf me. Maybe we'll be okay, I think to myself . . . maybe.

For once, I sing to Yoel. He tosses handfuls of rock salt and mint leaves into my bath, and I sing Patsy Cline to him. His ears bristle like a watchdog discerning danger in everyday noise, and after several bars of "Walkin' after Midnight" and "Sweet Dreams," we both realize I'm singing America—romantic, lonely, and dangerously convinced of its own good intentions. In Cuba, Yoel's a musician. What will he be in the United States? Just another black man? He's too proud to take jobs repairing air conditioners or climbing ladders. How will I feed him?

These questions race through my mind, but for now, we're up, show-ered, dressed, and sputtering toward the airport in an unofficial taxi. At the checkout counter, a bored ticket agent takes one look at us and asks Yoel if he'll be traveling with me. He glowers. She smirks. I put my suit-case on the carousel and hand him my last five dollars.

The intercom is blaring out the details of the flight in an urgent, hyperbolic tone, imploring all passengers to report to the gate imme-diately. We hurry toward the yellow line that marks the entrance to the booths one must enter in order to exit Cuba. We hug and I start to walk toward the booth, then Yoel does something extraordinary. He steps over the yellow line and enters the booth with me. Cubans never cross the line that divides those who are staying from those who are leaving. Shoulder-to-shoulder, we occupy the width of the stuffy booth. An older man with a five o'clock shadow looks up in surprise. Yoel's chest is strong and proud through his perfectly pressed T-shirt. His jawline is firm and his face scowls slightly, the way he does when he feels threatened. The man's large brown eyes sag with age and fatigue. I feel as if I'm no longer in the room. They stare at each other with familiarity and intimacy.

"Buenos días, compañero," the official breaks the silence.

Yoel's scowl relaxes for a few seconds of polite formality, "Hola."

"Your friend's heading back to . . ." his voice trails off as I hand him my passport and the tourist visa on a separate card. "Ah, the United States."

"Miami," Yoel corrects him. It's clear he hasn't decided to back down yet. He stands with his feet shoulder-width apart and his hands clasped behind his back like a referee.

"So how may I help you today, compañero?" The soldier stamps the card hastily and returns his unflinching gaze to Yoel. Silence. I shift my weight. Just as quickly as he entered the booth, Yoel's demeanor suddenly relaxes and he places his hand on my shoulder. "Just want to make sure she's well taken care of."

"Of course you do. Los Cubanos are still gentlemen, right? We take care of our women." Yoel smiles in agreement. Although I'm anx-ious to catch my plane, there's nothing I can do but wait out this exchange. It pretends to be all about my well-being and honor but really has nothing to do with me and everything to do with the two Cubans posturing at each other: Yoel, who cannot leave Cuba, and the guard, who cannot leave either but is in charge of reinforcing this repression however politely or violently he chooses. Yoel hugs me once again, says goodbye to the immigration official, and turns to leave. As I exit the booth on one side and he on the other he's a blur in my peripheral vision. But the metal door that locks behind him with a loud, industrial click is solid. Yoel *cannot* leave, but I can. I have the power he lacks.

Miami

I find a tiny studio apartment in an old Florida building on Miami Beach. Just off the 72nd Street Causeway, the two-story, peachy-pink stucco building is surprisingly still intact among the high-rises. The scabbed metal railing along the second floor makes it look more like a motel than an apartment building, but it's on the intercoastal waterway, and I have a corner studio on the first floor. When I unroll my thin Japanese mattress across its low wooden frame and lie down, I lie parallel to the ocean. When I sit up, the silvery water floats just below eye level.

I talk to lawyers. One Saturday afternoon, raising my voice over a whirling weed trimmer, I introduce myself to Bernie, the lawyer-neighbor of a friend. He wears cargo shorts frayed at the edges and a faded polo shirt. His three young children scrape out jagged drawings on the sidewalk with pastel chalks while his moon-faced South American wife plants azaleas in wooden flower boxes.

Bernie compares immigration to winemaking. He speaks of establishing the climate and conditions for certain privileges to take fruit and flourish. I try to imagine Yoel swelling and rounding out with residency, and after great patience and careful cultivation, finally arriving at citizenship. I'd never thought of citizenship as something one could hold up to the light in a large crystal goblet.

Bernie refers me to a more economical lawyer, a slight man with thinning dark hair who unconsciously twirls miniature Honduran and American flags in a cup on his desk while I tell him my story—how I met Yoel and why I want to bring him here. When I've finished, he rubs his temples wearily, looks down at the initial information form I'd filled out in the waiting room, and addresses me by my first name: "I've seen these cases," he sighs. "They usually end badly." Suddenly, I'm someone with "a case," and one that will probably end badly.

"I feel like I've been diagnosed with a terminal illness," I comment wryly. He laughs and adds that he'll help me file my case.

I buy twenty-dollar Mi Cuba! phone cards at the Western Union on 49th and Biscayne Boulevard, so that I can call Yoel. He doesn't have a phone, so each time we speak, he tells me when and where to call next. Sometimes it's his band manager's mother, Juanita, who gives him privacy, other times I phone the *casa particular* where a foreign student taking batá classes from him is staying. Yoel's days are filled with playing music, rustling up students for private lessons, and procuring food. Last week, he used his last two dollars on a taxi to get to a lesson on time, only to find the student had already left. He had to walk more than five miles to get home. These hard-luck stories abound, but Yoel rarely shares them with me.

I live close to the ground, eating against the wall. I hold the short stubs of candles brought from Cuba over the flame of a match until the wax melts, then push them into the center of a ceramic saucer on the floor. I can imagine Yoel in this room, playing his batá in the flickering light or coming in the door clutching a bunch of sunflowers, but I can't imagine him in the United States—the man with the insatiable appetite, the man who would want me never to go out with friends or walk alone, the man whose only real job has been playing music. In Cuba, when he walks down the street, people greet him by drumming their hands on the tops of cars, tabletops, and boxes. Here, will women clutch their purses closer as he approaches? Will Cubans look at him suspiciously until they hear him speak Spanish, and even then, will they treat him as a hustler, *un recién llegado*? I can't imagine life with him, but neither can I imagine being one of the people who disappears, forgets about him, and simply makes a new life, leaving him to suffer the daily humiliation of life in Cuba. During one of our conversations, I offhandedly mention that it would be easy for him to track down his father once he's here. "Really?" he asks in a defensive tone tinged with incredulousness. When I explain that he could just call directory assistance, get the number, and call his father, he falls silent. Maybe he is smarter than me: he knows better than to get burned, even for the promise of sweetness.

I won't commit to buying a writing tablet or new pen, but I've started writing again—random notes on loose sheets of paper. I go quietly about my business: writing, sleeping by the sea, and gathering evidence in a case for which among other exhibits—photos, letters of support, and a cashier's check—I need a copy of my birth certificate. One day, it arrives unexpectedly.

On my birth certificate there's a blank where my father's name should be. It's as if I were never born. I stare at the blank space—the stomachache of my childhood, the musky smell of the pretend uncle who once accompanied me to a father-daughter banquet, the empty seat at church, my mother's tired hand pushing me half-heartedly toward school, friends, and activities. I feel as if he never existed, as if I'd imagined him. I stare at the form until the spaces and print start to shift, and for a split second, I think my mother was a radical and put her name where my father's name should have been. My mother: radical, ahead of her time.

It's raining so we duck into John Martin's, an Irish pub in Coral Gables with brass fixtures, wood paneling, and dark beers. I'm with Liz, one of my closest friends in Miami. The place is as cold as a meat locker, and we're both shivering as we take a seat in one of the back rooms to avoid the noise at the bar. Liz looks at me with her wide, brown eyes and observes, "There's something different about you. Something from allá." I shrug and smile to myself, remembering that Alejandro had referred to Cuba with the same anonymous moniker. Even in 2000, people in Miami don't talk openly about going to or coming from Cuba.

A few weeks have gone by since I returned, and I've forgotten about the request I made of my closest friend that she make a call. So when Liz tells me my father is dead, the news startles me, even though I'd intuited it weeks ago. A dry, cracked sound erupts from my throat.

"Really?"

"Yes," Liz nods solemnly. A waitress passes by hefting a tray of dark bottles on her shoulder. My eyes well up, and I lower my head, rubbing my forehead with the heel of my hand.

I had wanted to know my father's whereabouts without the fear of his wife hanging up on me, so I asked Liz, born in Cuba, raised in Miami, to call her on my behalf. Liz is one of the few people who could deliver this news. She, too, met her father later in life. Her mother left Cuba when Liz was six months old, thinking her husband would soon join them, but he was jailed and didn't make it to Miami until the Mariel Boatlift more than a decade later. When he finally arrived, he was a broken man—silent, cruel, with a chunk of flesh missing from his bicep.

Only Liz could deliver this news, and in an act of friendship, she reports her conversation with Zoraida without censoring it or trying to make the news more palatable. In January, at the age of eighty-five, my father was admitted to the hospital with pneumonia; after a couple of weeks, he died there. Later, I'll check my journal for the exact date. On Saturday, January 29, the day my father died, I was reeling with nausea and dizziness in Havana.

"As soon as I told her who I was and why I was calling, she let out a big sigh," Liz says. "It was like she was relieved or something, like she'd been waiting for the call." Zoraida spoke in a sharp, wild voice, saying she didn't know why I was so obsessed with her husband. She went on and on, saying that now she was alone since they'd never had children.

"I would've opened up to her if he would have," Zoraida told Liz. "We were never even sure she was his daughter anyway." A pitcher of amber Guinness sloshes past our heads. Zoraida told Liz they had asked my mother for a paternity test, and she'd refused.

"Wow," I say.

Liz nods, "Wow."

Even though I know what she says about the paternity test isn't true, I'm shocked at the power Zoraida still has over me. Chills run through my body and I'm short of breath, like someone punched me hard in the stomach. How did I end up here again: the dial tone in my ear and Zoraida pretending she doesn't know who I am?

There will be no memorial service or last words. This is it: Liz putting her hand on mine. We leave the freezing bar and head over to El Pub, a cafeteria on Eighth Street, for a café con leche. In another country I could have walked all night and moved forward with this news. Here, I have to sit still with it. Liz looks tired, but she won't admit it until I let her know I'm okay. We finish our coffee, and she drops me off at my place.

That night, as I drift off to sleep in my little apartment by the sea, I think I can finally put him to rest. But the next morning, I wake up with a huge weight of sadness pressed down on my chest. I light a candle, walk outside, and stand close to the water, which is locked between the concrete patio that juts out from my apartment building and the steel girders of the causeway bridge. I slip on a pair of shoes and walk to the midpoint of the bridge, wanting to see the ocean's expanse, hoping it will make my grief feel smaller.

Staring at the ocean, slate-colored and moody beneath the low-hanging clouds, I remember the gray rim around the iris of Alejandro's brown eyes, always *almost* ready to take on their permanent color. I feel a twinge of regret. I let him down. I let Cuba's faulty phone lines and blackouts barricade me from saying a sincere goodbye to someone

I cared for. I know Alejandro is out there somewhere wishing me well, and to my surprise, I want the same for him.

Zoraida's words circled through my sleep all night, wrapping my wrists, neck, and fingers in the heavy lead necklace of her lies: *We were never even sure she was his daughter. We were never even sure. . . .* I don't think I ever realized how desperately she needed to deny my existence until now. It stretched beyond her relationship with my father. It stretched beyond my father's life even.

"No soy Adriana," I stammer into the receiver. "Who's Adriana?" I've phoned Yoel at our prearranged time, and when I announce myself as *la novia* to the foreign voice that answers the phone, I'm greeted as Adriana. I'm standing in my studio's kitchenette, which has a small window that looks onto the water. I feel my way past the kitchen counter to my futon and sit. The floor feels like it's rocking back and forth. My heart is racing.

"Who is Adriana? Who are you?" I demand, and the halting, indecipherable Spanish on the other line tells me he's sorry. It's a mistake. Wrong number. His accent doesn't belong to a European or an English speaker. It sounds Asian. I want to hang up, to scream, to throw the phone across the room, but even in my state of shock, I know that communication with Cuba is too precarious. A temper tantrum could cut contact irrevocably.

"Wait. Please, wait," I say slowly, calmly in the clearest, best-enunciated, ESL-teacher English I can muster. "Do you speak English?"

"Yes, little bit." He switches to almost equally incomprehensible English, but it's better than his Spanish, one less linguistic barrier to overcome.

"What's your name? Where are you from?"

Ryogi from Japan tells me his batá lesson ended fifteen minutes ago and Yoel promptly headed home. We'd agreed to talk at 2:00. My alarm clock glares 2:03. Our most recent communications had been uncharacteristically erratic. Over the last few weeks, Yoel had missed a few of my calls, but he'd apologized profusely the next time we spoke, and I'd not worried too much about these lapses. This time it was clear: he'd missed my call intentionally.

"I must to go. This not my house, not my phone," Ryogi stammers in a nervous, formal voice.

"Wait, Ryogi, please. I'm calling from the United States. I know you don't know me," I take a deep breath and try to control my tone. "Ryogi, I am bringing Yoel to the United States. We're engaged."

"Miss, really, I don't. . . ."

"Please," my voice cracks, betraying my sense of desperation, "anything you can tell me about Adriana would be very helpful."

Ryogi pauses, and I'm sure he'll hang up, but whether out of pity or courtesy, he doesn't. He says he doesn't know Yoel well. He only takes batá lessons with him, but Adriana is always with him, so he's always assumed she is his girlfriend. I thank him and hang up.

From the floor where I'm sitting, the silvery line of Florida's intercoastal waterway shines through my window at eye level, creating the illusion I'm on a raft. This tiny, one-room studio initially charmed me, but now I'm seeing it in a new way: my bed is a one-inch-thick futon mattress splayed carelessly across midnight blue indoor-outdoor carpet; unpacked boxes line the walls, even though I've lived here two months. I have no table or chairs, and my computer, my only possession of any value, is propped up on a sagging piece of plywood between two beige, metal file cabinets.

A couple of days later, an envelope arrives from the U.S. Immigration and Naturalization Service. Sure enough, the opening line glares: "Welcome to the United States of America. . . ." For a few seconds, I want to believe, as many before me have, that this letter is fortuitous, a sign of good things to come. Yoel can finally come to Miami.

Norma

I call the only other person who knew my father. I call my mother and tell her my father is dead.

It's between 6:00 and 6:30 p.m. Central Standard Time. I know this because my mother is watching *Wheel of Fortune*. After a pause, she says, "I'm very sorry, Sweetheart" and then, "Well, he was getting on in years." Her voice has an odd, unfamiliar ring to it. It's sweet, not saccharine exactly, but also uncharacteristically sweet considering she never had a kind word to say about my father when he was alive. Then I pinpoint it: she's polite. In the wake of my father's death, my mother is being polite. She's blissfully detached, as if he were someone only I had known and lost, and it ignites my temper.

Prompting wild, canned applause from the audience, Pat Sajak's booming voice announces the prize for the bonus round: a Caribbean cruise for two. All these years, whenever I've tried to express my feelings about not having a father, my mother's cut me off with one of her glib remarks or with full-throttle drama. If I cried, my mother could cry harder. If I grew silent, she held her silence longer. The game-show bells are dinging deliriously. My father has died and she doesn't even bother to turn down *Wheel of Fortune*. I jump to the attack.

"Mom," I accuse, "why didn't you even bother to put his name on my birth certificate?"

My mother sighs. Lynne from Sioux City, Iowa, calls out the letter *T* and Pat cheers, "One, two, three. You got three *T*'s, Lynne!"

"I don't know what you want me to say, Babe."

"Do you know what it's like having an incomplete birth certificate? That's just trippy, okay? That's just crazy." I sound like a teenager. I take a deep breath and try to steady myself. "It hurts, okay? That's what I'm trying to say." A row of unpacked boxes lines the wall in front of my futon, emitting the sweet dusty smell of cardboard.

"Oh, Baby," my mother sighs in a sad voice. Another contestant, a mother of two from Orange County, chirps that she's going to buy a vowel.

I take another deep breath. "It makes me feel like I was never born, like I'm no one."

Saying it out loud like that brings up a surge of emotion just below the surface. I put down the phone and pull my pillow in front of my chest, sobbing. My mother might break down and cry too, or she might hang up and later say, "I just wanted to give you some space." I'm aware of the possibilities. I've lived much of my life anticipating them, but I don't care. My chest heaves and I sob. I sob until my nose is running and my vision is blurred. Maybe for the first time, I sob beyond the fringes of how my mother may or may not react.

When I pick up the phone, she's still there. *Wheel of Fortune* is on mute.

"Do you know what the wife said, Mom?"

"What did she say?" Her voice is no longer sweet or conciliatory. It's almost neutral.

"She said they didn't even know if I was his daughter for sure."

"That was never a question," she says slowly, an undertone of anger seeping through her enunciation of "question."

"Why didn't you even put his name on the certificate, then?"

I know José was my father. I just don't understand why my mother made the choices she did. "Why were you so determined to do everything yourself? Why did we have to live like fugitives in that middle-of-nowhere town?" I put the phone down again. I don't care if she hears me. I don't care if she can cry harder than me or if she admonishes me in her newfound polite voice to call her back when I can "pull myself together." I collapse onto my mattress. The edges of papers and corners of boxes fall in my line of vision, only five or six inches away from my nose. They loom bigger than anything else in the apartment. I don't want to see any more certificates, forms, letters, or notes. I sob. I let myself cry until I'm quiet. I pick up the phone and clear my throat.

"I did put his name on the birth certificate," my mother says, her voice sober and grown-up sounding.

"Really?"

"Yes," she says in a matter-of-fact tone. "I wrote it right there with my name, and after a few minutes the RN on duty came back with a hospital administrator who told me, 'In these cases, we don't put anything.'"

When she says "in these cases" my mother enunciates a wry, elongated "these." For once, her punch line makes sense to me. Her telling is not defensive witty repartee. It has genuine emphasis and intention. In her pronunciation, she repossesses the bland pronoun "these" that hospital administrators long ago turned on her like a blade sharper than birth. After she'd struggled and labored and finally reached the early ecstasy of having delivered, an administrator deemed her delivery one of a select group of cases—"these" cases were invalid and unworthy of documentation. In a word, illegitimate. *Ilegítimo*, in Spanish or English means the same thing. This is one of the purest cognates I know.

"I even tried to get a lawyer," my mother announces. Her molasses cadence is simple and serious, not tinged with its characteristic helplessness. My mother goes on to recount that when she told the lawyer about the incident at the hospital where they wouldn't let her put José's name on the birth certificate, he said, "Well, these situations can get pretty messy. You probably shouldn't do anything." Again, the vindictive "these."

I know the rest: my mother, a single woman alone, exhausted from giving birth and needing to get back to work, does the next best thing. She returns to her job, says nothing of the hospital incident, and tells people she's a widow.

"I wrote to your father and told him you were precious," she adds. "I sent him a picture of you. I was really struggling and asked him for help. He said the only time I'd see him would be in court."

She's never told me this. Her attitude has always conveyed that my father wanted nothing to do with us, but now she says it. She matches a narrative to her tone.

"The last time I talked to your father, I cried. He hated crying and said we couldn't talk on the phone anymore. That was the last time we spoke until the day I called you at his house in Miami."

My mother has always said it was her call to Miami that infuriated Zoraida and ruined my chances of having a relationship with my father. It's true. That was the day when cabinet doors slammed in the bright, white kitchen and my father held the phone out to me with a ghostly expression on his face. That was the moment when our relationship drastically changed course. Zoraida threw a fit and barricaded my father from all communication with me thereafter. It would be easy to blame my mother's call, and for many years I did. But my mother's story prompts something I'd forgotten.

Later that day, surrounded by Zoraida's sewing supplies, I cried helplessly and bitterly. My father knelt next to my bed. I glared at him.

I had scheduled my trip knowing my birthday would fall in the midst of it and hoping he might remember it. I'd so fluently blended with his food and language that when my birthday began to unfold like any other day, it threw me back into the reality that my father was a stranger. I lay on the bed crying, detached, and listless. My father knelt beside me, peered at me through his psychiatrist's spectacles, and observed: "Today you are twenty, but you have the maturity of a twelve-year-old."

I'd always secretly blamed myself—certain that my crying and immaturity were what pushed him away. I realize now that he was incapable of seeing tears. He kept my photo all those years. He romanticized me, but at the first sign of emotion, he pulled away as he had done with my mother and probably with many others.

My mother didn't call intending to sabotage my relationship with my father. She didn't even call to tell him that day was my birthday. She called to be recognized. She wanted to be acknowledged. So did I. My mother did flee to a strange town and a new life, but for the first time, I see her as not merely running away, but also as being pushed away—and finally, pushing back.

"Can I tell you something about my first marriage?" she asks.

"Yes, but let me call you back," I say, wanting to wash my face and get a drink of water first. Then thinking the better of it, I say: "Never mind, Mom. Tell me."

One Sunday in 1954, after dinner, my mother slipped on a simple white gold band with a marquis diamond set in the center and submerged her hands in the sudsy dishwater. Jerry, a doctor she was dating, sat in the front room making stiff small talk with her parents. When her mother came in to help dry, Norma Jewel rinsed away the foamy cloud and held out her hand. Her mother howled and broke a plate. "You're not going to marry that Negro!" Jerry, or Jerónimo, Leonin was a resident on his way to becoming a surgeon. He was Filipino and Catholic. My mother's parents were poor, white, and staunchly Protestant.

When my mother's mother emerged, having taken to her bed for a few days as if in mourning, she cried. "It's enough to give me a heart attack—you marrying that nasty black thing!" she wailed.

"You'd better not go then," my mother replied in a nonchalant tone.

"Your father won't give you away in the Catholic Church," her mother threatened. "He's a deacon in the Methodist Church."

"Fine. I can walk down the aisle myself," my mother responded.

And she did. It was 1954 when she walked down the aisle of St. James Catholic Church alone. She wore a white lace tea-length gown with seed pearls stitched into the bodice and carried a bouquet of pink rosebuds. She became Mrs. Jerry Leonin. All of this alone, without the blessing of her parents. In the end, it wasn't such a leap for my mom to raise me alone. She wasn't trying to escape my father. She was escaping the wrath of her family. She'd been walking down the aisle alone for a long time.

My mother is Norma. In Spanish, *norma* means rule, norm, law. She is the law given and the law broken. My mother wasn't a radical, but she did radical things. She raised a Leonin in a town of Smiths and Joneses. She had a traditional Catholic wedding where she walked herself down the aisle. She planted us deep in the Heartland and dutifully worked as a nurse in order to feed, clothe, and educate me, but she also whipped up exotic cocktails in her blender. She burned candles and incense and told stories of dancing the rumba, mambo, and cha-cha-cha with foreign men. She broke the rules but remained profoundly bound to them.

A couple of days later, a plain manila envelope arrives in the mail. No note, just my address in my mother's elegant script on the outside and two documents inside. I immediately recognize these as objects I'd uncovered in an old box when I was a child hunting treasure in the basement. The couple of times I'd discovered them, my mother had snatched them away and launched into a long bout of sobbing.

I sit down on my futon and examine the yellow laminated birth record. The first story of my birth—that Jerry Leonin was my father and he died—begins with this document. I'm not sure how my mother managed it, but she got someone to put his name on an altered version of my birth certificate. She used this to enroll me in school, but more importantly, it cemented the story that my father was dead.

Perhaps she had planned on telling me the truth about José, but seeing the document, it made the story much less complicated and difficult to tell. I think the sting of her parents' rejection of her marriage with Jerry never completely wore off. Even hundreds of miles and decades away, she was still walking down the aisle alone, spiting her parents yet never quite breaking the hold they had on her.

The other document is a photo of my father, stamped May 29, 1965, just four days short of two years before I would be born. He looks dapper in his gray suit jacket, white pressed shirt, and dark tie. His thick dark brown hair is slicked back. The large hazel eyes and wide forehead that I recognized the first day we met are even more clearly identical to mine in this younger rendering of him.

I turn the photo over and see the labored cursive of my youth. I'm sure I copied out the message over and over before writing on the back of the photo in an attempt to tame my indecipherable, jagged script into something elegant and controlled. The back of the photo reads: "In undying love for the memory of my beloved father Jerry Leonin. As ever, your loving daughter, Mia Angela Leonin. Age 15½ January 31, 1982."

Even though I was only a few months shy of sixteen when I wrote it, I read this message now and see in it a child's logic. I wrote the note in the way I would have wanted my father to write it if he had dedicated the photo to me. A small voice in me was surfacing, claiming unconditional faithfulness to this stranger, hoping he would return the same. I don't see the sentiment of a girl who lost her father. I see a girl trying to believe something about her father, anything.

In less than six months, my mother will break down and tell me my father is not her former husband, Jerry Leonin, the man who died many years before. My father is José Ignacio Alsina, a doctor from Cuba. "He didn't want anything to do with the birth," my mother will cry. I'll console her. We'll wash our faces, go out for ice cream, and say nothing more about the incident for many years.

Yemayá

There's a photo from that first trip, taken in 1988, the day after my father picked me up at the airport. In the snapshot, I'm sitting on the screened-in porch off the guest room. It's a close-up of the back of my head and shoulders. I'm wearing a red-and-white striped bathrobe and scribbling something in a writing tablet. I rediscovered it the other day when, in search of paper, I opened an unpacked box.

And there were more peculiar photos taken surreptitiously from odd angles: my hair wrapped in a large, white towel as I sat at the breakfast bar where we ate all our meals; my elbow as I dip my spoon into a parfait glass of arroz con leche; my head bent over a book; my handwriting; the V of my hair at the base of my neck. At the end of my visit, my father developed duplicate copies of all the photos we'd taken and gave me a set.

I'd always thought these were taken by mistake, but I could never throw them away. Now I realize my father took these pictures intentionally. He wanted glimpses of me from every angle. Lately, I've asked myself the unimaginable: what was it like for him to meet me? How did it feel having me in his home—this moody, charming, English-speaking, female version of himself, this intimate stranger. I have no answers except that I must have been a mystery to him too.

I'm rattling down the causeway in my '93 Honda with Yoel's letter of permission. A metal coffee can is strapped into the passenger seat. I park in the public library parking lot on Collins Avenue and head toward the ocean. Crossing over the rickety boardwalk, I notice a Cuban émigré has scrawled Alafia (blessings) on the splintered wood of the railing. It's a March afternoon. The wind whips wildly, and only a few devoted sunbathers are scattered on the beach. A transistor radio squeaks in the high winds, along with the squawking gulls.

I stand before the waves and light a fire under the letter, lowering it into the can long enough for it to catch flame. I stand at the shore with the letter burning in my hand. The wind blows the flame wildly, and at the last second before it burns my hand, I drop the letter and its contents into the can. I give Yoel's permission to enter the United States to the sea. It doesn't matter who Adriana is. Yoel doesn't belong to me. He never did. I thought if Yoel and I shared the same pain, we couldn't hurt each other. I was wrong. As I leave, I plant the can of ashes firmly in the sand and sea grass below the railing. Alafia.

I go home, park my car, and walk to my favorite place at the top of the causeway bridge. The ocean is moving. The ocean is always moving. Wherever we are at any given moment, the colors are churning: purple crashes to violet; turbulent gray swirls deepen to charcoal; white foamy peaks crest benignly and vanish.

Having been on both sides, I now believe that the ocean does join bodies of land, that something exists beyond the choppy, gray surface and the thin line of horizon.

I believe there's a mother or some being that presides over these divisions and unions of people and the lands they populate. I know some people who call her Yemayá; I saw her dancing, her skirts whirling. I believed in her because she had multiple sides—fierce and angry, calm and compassionate, peaceful and proud. I scream "Yemayá!" but the fierce winds muffle my voice. I scream her name again and again, louder each time. It's lost as soon as it escapes my lips.

It feels exhilarating and comforting to scream into something bigger than myself, for my most forceful voice to be small and insignificant. The fire of my voice scorches my throat. My voice passes over like a fire, turning to ashes all I asked and didn't ask, all I was told and not told. I want to let it burn to the center, so that I can speak new truths and tell new stories.

For many years, I thought Zoraida was the obstacle between my father and me. That if I could just get past Zoraida, he would see me and embrace me as his daughter. Then I thought that if I could learn Spanish, if I could know his island, he would love me. Even when I intuited that my father was gone, I still dreamed of returning and speaking Spanish with him. If I could speak Spanish, his wife couldn't hang up on me.

I put my faith in language to reconcile us. If I could translate my questions into his language or translate him into my language, we'd be close. If I could speak the language of his heart, maybe he could find a place for me there, but the heart doesn't know a language. Willingness, not language, is the precondition for dialogue.

I've been waiting quite some time now—waiting alone in my room of unpacked boxes, stubs of candles on chipped saucers, papers flattened under my mattress, my computer balanced on a sagging plank of plywood. I need somewhere to write. I need a place to eat. Tomorrow, I will call a friend to go out and share a simple meal. Tomorrow, I'll start looking for a table and chair.

About the Author

Mia Leonin is the daughter of a Cuban immigrant and a Louisville native. She is the author of two books of poetry: *Braid* and *Unraveling the Bed*, both published by Anhinga Press.

Leonin's poetry and nonfiction have been published in *New Letters*, *Indiana Review*, *North American Review*, *Prairie Schooner*, *Chelsea*, and *Witness*. She's been awarded an Academy of American Poets Prize and is the recipient of a 2005 Florida Individual Artist Fellowship.

Leonin has written extensively on Spanish-language and Hispanic theater, dance, and culture for the *Miami Herald*, *Miami New Times*, and other periodicals. She's the recipient of a Green Eyeshade Award for theater criticism and was selected as a fellow in the NEA/Annenberg Institute on Theater and Musical Theater.

Leonin holds an MFA from the University of Miami, where she is a full-time creative writing instructor.